THE MILE HIGH CLUB

I0803033

DANIELLE STYRON & JAMES STYRON

THE MILE HIGH CLUB

confessions of a _private_ jet _flight_ attendant

Post Hill Press

A POST HILL PRESS BOOK
ISBN: 979-8-89565-018-9
ISBN (eBook): 979-8-89565-019-6

The Mile High Club:
Confessions of a Private Jet Flight Attendant
© 2025 by Danielle Styron and James Styron
All Rights Reserved

Cover design by Danielle Styron

This book, as well as any other Post Hill Press publications, may be purchased in bulk quantities at a special discounted rate. Contact orders@posthillpress.com for more information.

All people, locations, events, and situations are portrayed to the best of the author's memory. While all of the events described are true, many names and identifying details have been changed to protect the privacy of the people involved.

No part of this book may be reproduced, stored in a retrieval system, or transmitted by any means without the written permission of the author and publisher.

Post Hill Press
New York • Nashville
posthillpress.com

Published in the United States of America
1 2 3 4 5 6 7 8 9 10

For anyone who's ever felt like money
would solve all their problems

TABLE OF CONTENTS

WELCOME ABOARD

Indulge your inner voyeur and join us in the private jet cabins of the wildly rich and uber-famous.

This book is a delicious collection of true stories featuring billionaire bullies, the people who enable them, and internationally recognized celebrities—as they truly are. You don't know just how audacious, cringe-worthy, and incomprehensible the 1 percent can be.

But, baby…you will.

Names have been changed to protect (us from) the malevolent.
Behaviors have been presented to humble them.
You know who you are.

Sit down, fasten your seatbelt, and grab that oxygen mask. Someone will be by with drinks soon…I recommend something stiff.

Secure the cabin for takeoff.

Welcome to *The Mile High Club*.

CHAPTER 1

GREAT SEXPECTATIONS

The phone rings. Finally. It's happening. I've been on the one-yard lines of many, many pilots, ever since I finished my six-day intensive training program.

And today, I can't believe it, someone is *CALLING ME* about a full-time job! I am beaming. I am untouchable. I am levitating. I am drafting an acceptance speech that will be delivered to millions on some sort of cable news network, a Breaking Broadcast for Bad Bitches. I am every woman kicking out the glass ceiling and rising to new heights.

It's about fucking time.

A few things to keep in mind about the Private Aviation industry:

1) Considering the seven weeks of paid training commercial Flight Attendants receive, private aviation is basically the Wild West.
2) Generally speaking, there are two kinds of training courses you can enroll in. They're both "legitimate," but one is like going Ivy League and the other is like

attending a fourth-tier law school in the Caribbean. I may or may not have had the Caribbean experience first. The Ivy League involves getting sprayed in the face with water jets (to simulate a water rescue) and learning how to spit roast lizards on deserted islands. For food. Yeah. Survival shit. I did them both, but I only brag about one.

3) The people who fly private are some of the most privileged human beings that have ever set foot on the face of the earth. Their ranks include some very happy, very friendly people—but contain far more brooding, miserable vampires of human joy.

Does that sound dramatic?

You don't know the half of it, sister.

After completing two very different (very expensive) courses to become, ahem, "certified," I found out there are three main categories of private flights.

There's Part 91. That's when you *own* the jet. Your pilots fly however far for however long you choose. Ditto for Flight Attendants. Their world, their rules.

Then there's Part 135. This is when you *rent* the jet. The specifics are hammered out ahead of time, and crews are offered the job. Because of all the legalities involved in renting, you are largely bound by more regulations of the FAA, however scant they may be. It means you can't overwork the staff, for the most part.

Finally, there's Part 125. This is when you're in a group of twenty or more, like a professional sports team. It's also a rental, often rented by the year, not by the trip, and so it's forced to follow similar regulations as 135s.

So besides learning how to pour a Diet Coke in turbulence and how to pop the doors off an aircraft, there aren't a lot of basic qualifications to fly Part 91. It's no rules—or more accurately, house rules.

And there aren't usually a ton of them.

But in that moment, as my phone rang and my heart raced, I didn't really understand the depth of this. I just knew I was fucking pumped—and relieved.

Not least of all because I'd used the last three thousand dollars in my bank account to put myself through Corporate Aviation a.k.a. Private Flight Attendant School. As I said, there are a few to choose from, all of which have varying degrees of legitimacy. In a private industry like this one with limited oversight, the environment is rife with scam operations like the first school I attended. Some were upwards of five thousand dollars. There was no way I could come up with that kind of bread.

In fact, I'd been forced to give up on my city life after a fire drove me out of my perfect apartment—within a month of moving into it. Big thanks to gas companies for not giving a fuck what unlicensed pricks do to company pipes.

When the call came in, I was scrolling through LinkedIn from my childhood bed, finding yet more pilots to bombard with eager messages about joining their team.

But perhaps no more! The call was a number I'd already saved: a pilot I'd already connected with on LinkedIn. I made almost all of my aviation connections there. But back then, the fact that I, with no actual experience flying anyone, was being considered for even a test flight sent my floundering self-esteem through the roof.

His message from the day before said they were looking for full-time staff, and I couldn't control my excitement. The best

I could do was let the phone ring a few times to not appear too thirsty.

I answered. He launched into a friendly pitch.

The exact language of our first call is hazy. I remember him being very confident and full of promises. He said he loved my look and vibe.

Professionally it was kind of weird. Personally, it's not unusual for me to hear.

We had an easy, friendly chat for about fifteen minutes. He confirmed that he was the full-time pilot, and the job was for a Part 91 account.

And, most importantly, he wanted to confirm that I was available to interview for the full-time role.

I could have backflipped. Hell yes I'm available!

We set a time for a formal interview and hung up a few minutes later.

I was shocked. Nope—I was freaking out.

My first interview, bitches. What, like it's hard?

* * *

There's an idiom (that I hate) about putting your eggs in a single basket. I mean I get it, but I think I heard it so much growing up that I subconsciously rebelled against it.

I'm an investor. I try not to be. But I am. I love it. I get invested in people and events. It's not bad to form attachments—the fact that a lot of people can't make any makes me feel kind of like a superhero.

But when it comes to jobs...let's just say I might be permanently jinxed from sharing the details of job prospects before they've come through.

Or before all the details are clear.

But overall, I'm proud to be an eager beaver.

Again today, not wanting to seem too eager, I let his call ring a couple times. I mean, am I jobless? Yes. Flat broke? Also, yes. Living with my parents? YES!

This is starting to feel like a personal attack.

Am I legitimately desperate for work? Again, yes! BUT, am I still too-cool-for-school to answer the phone on the first ring?

Only on the outside.

I am having coffee with the family when my phone rings, about a minute before our scheduled call.

Nice. Prompt. I can get *on board* with that, pardon the pun.

I excuse myself from the parentals and answer with what feels like a million butterflies in my stomach. I now know it by its real name, say it with me, "anxiety." Why wasn't I this nervous last night?

"Hey Danielle, thanks for making time to talk."

The voice on the other end of the line comes through bright, crisp, and relaxed. It's the same confident friendliness as before, easy and open. His candidness immediately put my anxiety at bay.

"We're a really easy going crew," he says, "and we go on incredible bucket list trips all over the world. South Africa, Australia, Europe, you name it. Plus, the owner has a few estates around the US we visit.

"Oh and everything is covered on the trips including as much as you can eat and drink. We are strictly drug free, though."

I am scratching out notes as quickly as I can on a notepad I'd set up in the other room. Loving it, loving all of it. It's like one long list of "pros."

"We travel about twice a month."

Wow—that's it?! *That's barely part time hours.* My lizard brain screams *SIX MONTHS VACATION! DO IT! DO IT!*

He continues, "The owner's family is on the plane for about half the trips."

He waits a beat.

"He has a bit of an alternative lifestyle."

He waits another longer, lingering beat. The pause feels like it's stretching out into infinity.

"So his girlfriends fly the second trip of the month."

And *there* it is.

But who am I to judge? Maybe he and his wife have an arrangement. You never know. And I'm not Angel of the Prudes over here. I have gay and straight friends in non-traditional relationships, and open relationships are far more common than you'd think in the upper echelons of monied America. The one thing I take away from it: Love very rarely looks how you imagined it.

The pilot continues.

"The owner is very religious, incredibly low maintenance, and one of the nicest men on the planet. His friends call him [REDACTED] because he's so sweet to everyone and is genuinely a great person. Oh, and he doesn't drink or do any drugs of any kind."

Sober, you say. I guess everybody gets their rocks off in a different way. Addictions to drugs and alcohol are like addictions to food, or sex, or porn. They're used to fill a hole somewhere on the inside. They're all born from a craving to escape; some people do it with cannabis, some people do it with Little Debbie, and some people do it on Snapchat.

Sober people just fill their Vice Hole with something that doesn't come in a bottle, a box, or a baggie. So I'm not judging him in the least. I'm in the middle of an out-of-body experience, and all these details are just fine-tuning the color saturation. Seriously, am I dreaming right now?

And the religion thing...I'm not sure what I was imagining. A low key *Righteous Gemstones* situation, or a richer, nimbler Pat Robertson.

Honestly, I breeze past it.

Religious fanatics are everywhere; if you had his kind of money, you'd probably pick a God to thank, too (if you haven't already). It offers up the convenience of "blaming" your success on some kind of "grand plan," which follows that all your actions, good or bad, are covered by a holy insurance plan. Cheating on your wife becomes condoned by virtue of the fact that you are the one cheating, and you were blessed with the gifts that enable it. So it's a "slip up," or an "accident," or better, a "sign" that things aren't right, or (my favorite) "an opportunity to learn and grow." Religion can be a sword and a shield, but mostly it's a Rorschach test: whatever you want it to be.

As demonstrated here.

There is more, so much more.

"We've had our last Flight Attendant for more than a decade. She was a barista making his coffee one day in this little coffee shop."

He laughs. "He hired her right there on the spot. And the only reason she's leaving is because she's having children with her *husband*."

His chipper air sours a bit on the last sentence, like the smell of a passing trash truck from an apple orchard. And just as quickly, it's gone again.

"She is crushed to be leaving. She had such fun with this job. By the way, there is no uniform so she got to wear whatever she wanted and would even dress up in costumes depending on where they were going. She really had fun with the job—and on the job! We want to hire someone who would enjoy that, too."

Me. I would enjoy that, all of that, thank you. Dressing up? Mentally I land on the Britney-meets-Barbie-meets-Pan-Am spectrum (with…crucifixes?) but hey, projects evolve.

And so do living situations.

"You can live anywhere you want to. It won't matter. We'll fly you in for trips, no problem. We all live scattered across the US anyway. Go nuts."

Say what?! How is this job even available? Isn't there a shortlist? Looking back, the lack of competition for the position should have tipped me off. Even minimum wage jobs have competition; suffice to say, the salary range for this job was… more. Wouldn't they have someone in mind for it already? A recommendation?

But I resist the urge to ask. Our conversation lasted for *ninety minutes* and I wasn't about to scrap all that rapport over a question I, on some level, knew would lead to answers I didn't want to hear. Ninety minutes is unheard of in aviation. I have never again had an interview that lasted as long as my first interview with this owner's pilot. Time is money, and for crews, downtime is a rare, precious resource, not to be squandered. He wouldn't be investing this much effort if I wasn't a serious contender.

Like a good sitcom, we end on a high note. We will follow up the next day. He wants me to marinate on the job for a night, do my own research on the client, and decide if I am interested. If so, we'll talk salary numbers and the benefits package on call three.

I play it engaged and intrigued, but noncommittal. As we hang up, I am sure my rouse of calmness is a success.

Now I am free to sing and yell and dance around my confused parents. When I fill them in, they jump up and dance with me—had I proved their doubts were misplaced? That I would finally have a job they could brag about? That I was moving out soon?

Well…it's possible I left out a few extra-marital details. But come on—isn't there a limit to how much you share with *your* parents? Is it really anyone else's business who this person does or does not have sex with? And wouldn't my parents, who never met a judgement they couldn't pass, just focus on that, as opposed to the sobriety, or the travel, or the vacation time? They are beaming with pride—what kind of daughter would I be to take that away from them?

* * *

Now, I'm not sure how many of you have ever had to perform a salary negotiation. I've been in quite a few myself, and I find them to be a huge source of stress. I'd rather not talk about money. Offer me what's fair for being the kickass Flight Attendant that I am; what's the problem?

Can't we all just get along while looking at the world through expensive sunglasses?

But in all seriousness, can we stop salary-fucking people?

The next day, here he is again, right on time—his punctuality is unlike any client I will have over the next six years. He's cheerful again, bubbling over with affirmations and radiating positivity. He's ready to give me more details about the job, "if I'm still interested."

Oh, fuck, did I play it *too* aloof?

Very interested, I quickly affirm.

He chuckles knowingly.

I said it too fast. Oh no. I'm gonna say something stupid to try to cover it. Here it co—

"Danielle, I love how open you are. Open-minded. You're the kind of person who sees life differently. I'm glad you aren't thrown by the fact that he has a couple of girlfriends."

I'd lived in New York, I reassure him. It's not my place to judge. That's why we all have autonomy, so we can live our lives the way that please us.

"Exactly. Happy you feel that way. This job obviously requires *extreme* discretion. We don't talk to his wife about any of his trips when she flies with us...and we never answer any of her questions."

Oh. That seems kind of weird.

"Well," he continues, possibly spurred on by my non-response, "we think she's catching on that when he flies the second time in the month, it's more than just business."

Ohhh, okay. Pieces coming together. So they *don't* have an arrangement. Well. Okay. That feels icky. But my lizard brain is coming in hot with justifications and theories of self-determination. Not my life. Not my business.

He quickly moves on.

"And there's another part of the job I think you'll enjoy," he starts with a twinkle in his voice. "There are loads of opportunities to make money here. Not only do we pay six figures, but since he's a developer, you'll have the opportunity to sell properties on the side for him as well. Our last Flight Attendant made almost half a million dollars last year."

Six figures, plus commish? What's that, like five percent? Are you fucking kidding me?! Look at me summoning shit like a Ouija master! Part-time work, full-time pay. This is my home now. This reality is where I live.

"Yeah, man, it's a great job. I've been working for him for sixteen years and I will never leave."

He somehow still isn't finished. "Also, the owner is really into helping you make a better life. For all his staff. If you ever choose to go back to school, he'll foot the whole bill, as long as you keep above a 3.5 GPA."

Daddy Warbucks is out here turning women into physicists while I'm calculating shoe allowance and which city suits my complexion the most. I'm a monster, judge me.

But also, as a medical professional who left an industry to pursue this line of work, I'm extremely interested in this kind of program. I hear great things about the University of Miami...

He's still going. "Basically you get full benefits when you sign on, right from day one. There's no three-month wait, no weird clauses."

Pregnant beat.

"We should talk more about what life on the road would be like, if that's something you'd like to do?"

ABSOFUCKINGLUTELY.

"When we travel with the girlfriends, *those* trips are the really *fun* trips."

Oh yeah? The emphasis here sets off a sixth sense.

"Absolutely. Oh, they're all incredibly romantic destinations. One of his girlfriends is extremely high profile, so we have to be very discreet, anywhere and everywhere we go as I'm sure you can imagine. Which means we always stay at luxury properties—think dream destinations."

I'm curious about how the pilot's partner (wife, turns out) feels about him working in that kind of environment, so I ask him pretty straightforwardly. Is his significant other ever allowed to join him in these places?

He laughs a little. "I'm actually in the middle of a divorce," he says, side-stepping the question. I congratulate him—what else can you say? Have you ever met anyone who got divorced because they were happy?

"Thanks. I'm okay with it." Then he pivots. "You want to see a picture of our current Flight Attendant?"

Yes and of course. When am I *ever* going to turn down an opportunity to do some opposition recon? Granted, she's not direct competition, but I'll be attempting to fill shoes she's been standing in for years. Every piece of information helps.

He sends a picture. It's a recent pic but...girlfriend is straight out of the '80s. Not that it's a bad thing—the '80s had resurfaced in fashion, music, and pop culture.

Still, I am mildly confused. You could imagine her working at a coffee shop, her friendly face spinning an iPad around for your signature (and tip?). She's definitely cute, but she's....well, I must not be seeing the *je ne sais quoi* that got her Gisselle-ed out of a drive-thru window. I'm aware that, despite my attempts to remain nonjudgmental, my Judge Cup runneth over—suck it, I'm doing my best here. *I* didn't dress her like a Slavic hipster. And I'm only human.

"So, you don't mind traveling—that's great—and I love how open-minded you are. Let's talk a little more about that. There are some parts of the job that require an even more extreme level of discretion than we've talked about thus far."

Okay...more discrete than total silence about his comings and doings?

Beat.

"Do you have a boyfriend or a girlfriend?"

I recently ended a relationship as well, a fact I share with a touch of hesitation. He had voluntarily told me about his divorce; I didn't think you were allowed to ask job candidates personal questions like this. It's up there with "do you plan to have a baby" and "what's your ethnicity." That's not to say people *don't* ask—they're just not supposed to.

I'm single and straight.

"How straight?"

At this point, we've basically careened out of the professional world and directly into my bedroom. *That's a weird fucking question*, my lizard brain offers, which is scary considering it recognizes only fear and desire.

Pretty straight.

On the Kinsey Scale, this bitch registers at One. A hard one. No experimenting in college, no unexplored feelings. Proud ally (I regularly attend Pride) but securely heterosexual.

"Oh. Well...okay."

He sounds....disappointed...with that answer?

Since we're apparently way passed being coy, I bluntly ask him why he's asking me this.

A low chuckle comes through the line.

"So I keep telling you I like how open-minded you are because this job is an extreme alternate lifestyle. He is a very religious guy and that's why he has two girlfriends."

If you're keeping score at home, you'll notice he's referred to my "open-mindedness" no less than five times over three phone calls. And yes, I caught it, too.

I am definitely not following. Everything I know about Christianity, literally every denomination I can think of at this point, does not green-light girlfriends.

"The girlfriends will get down and dirty on the plane together so he can watch."

Fucking what?

"But, he is just a voyeur. He *never* touches them. *Ever*. He's a religious man, like I said."

So religious.

"He never touches them and he has a phrase that he uses to kind of get the party started."

A bible passage, I assume.

"Are you into girls at all? Our last Flight Attendant was straight too, but she would play with the girlfriends and he seemed to really like that."

There it is. Ole Coffee Katarina over there wasn't plucked from the crowd for no reason—she had a particular skill set that included vaginal diving, spectator spelunking, and the sexplo-oral arts. She was one of the women who made sexuality seem like something that could be flipped like a pancake. Also, don't zealots hate homosexuality? Is it different if you're gay for pay or is muff-diving a blessed exception?

And that's not even my biggest problem with the pitch!

I sit in silence while he keeps talking, seemingly unaware he'd lost the audience.

"Yeah, it's cool, you can drink as much as you want to get in the mood. It's just that he *really* likes the Flight Attendant to be into the girls and he'll know immediately if you're not. He wants passion. He wants to see you excited about it. He'll definitely know if you're not."

Yeah, because I'm *so* concerned about faking an orgasm for this crucifix-wielding hypocrite.

"And, you know, we only fly them once a month, so it's not like you have to be a lesbian, you would just need to have *fun* with them."

Hearing you loud and clear, bud.

And screaming on the inside.

I mean, OF FUCKING COURSE, right? There's no such thing as a free lunch. And the catch on his job is liable to strip me naked and force-feed me clam baskets.

But wait—there's more!

"How do you feel about *me*?"

Oookay, what's happening here? Nope, I totally know what's happening, and I'm totally doing my best to actively avoid it.

He's being super honest, friendly, and open, I express.

"Good, because when we're at our destination he likes to have *me* get into the mix, with the girls. He *really* likes to watch me fuck the Flight Attendant."

What in the Wife Swap is happening right now?!

The Flight Attendant is there to serve you food and drinks and save your life in case of an emergency. I must have missed the pamphlet on fucking your coworkers…and how are we *this* far into the interview and he's just bringing it up?

The answer to that is pretty obvious, actually. This isn't the kind of responsibility you list on monster.com. It's why he was willing to dump an hour and a half into our first phone call—return on investments, baby.

But I'm morbidly fascinated…SO MANY QUESTIONS.

Does he wear condoms?

"No. We all are tested regularly. Kind of part of the job."

STD tests.

Part. Of. The. Job.

What does his soon to be ex-wife think?

"Well, she doesn't know. It's like I said, you know, this job requires extreme confidentiality."

Wow. What's "the phrase" that kicks off this Lovefest?

"'Let's Party.'"

The catchphrase of hot girls in bathroom stalls all around Los Angeles. Incredible, and so unique.

What does the Flight Attendant's husband think?

"Oh, he doesn't know either. He never knew anything. Extreme discretion, remember?"

I really do.

Does the other pilot get tagged in?

"Nah. He's a slam clicker."

> Slam Clicker (slæm • klik-er)
>
> A flight crew member who gets to the destination only to slam and lock the hotel room door, never to be seen again until the crew rides back to the airport together.

Color me shocked. So not everyone on the team sees everyday as Humpday. The other pilot is just there for the paycheck, eh? Nice to know not every six-figure staffer is expected to use what's between their legs to stay competitive. I guess.

I really, *really* thought about it: Was I willing to sell out my sexuality to get out of my parents' house and possibly put some serious money away?

Was it worth it?

Would *you* do it?

I fire another seventy questions at him, but let's be honest, I'm pretty sure this is not the job for me. I'm just not that good of an actor. And, since apparently that counts, I'm disqualifying myself.

I make a few comments to that effect but they don't seem to land. He asks me directly if I'd be willing to have sex with a handful of women—women I would basically introduce myself to by sitting on their faces—as a routine part of the job. The quality of the question has grown more pointed. In reality, he's attempting to *confirm* that it's okay, "because you're so open-minded."

So, gingerly, I lay it out for him. As tempting as it is to go part-time vagitarian to get on payroll, I just don't think it's gonna work out. My face has a mind of its own and chronically betrays me.

Honestly, a resting bitch face would be better for the job. Plus, I truly cannot imagine in what world I would do all the grunt work of getting a plane ready, serving everyone onboard sashimi, and then having to eat *their* sashimi after cleaning up their dirty plates and refilling drinks. It's giving two jobs for the price of one.

Then I have to land, clean the plane up, and dive back into the fish tank once at the "romantic destination." Pick a struggle: I can either eat it or serve it, but to think I'd do both for single pay is the real crime here. Also, did I mention I'm pretty strictly dickly?

Sorry, a-hem, let me repeat that:

I SAID I WOULD CONSIDER CUNNILINGUS

OUT LOUD

IN A CORPORATE JOB INTERVIEW

Why the fuck did I take ballet instead of acting lessons.

* * *

As we wind up this heartwarming segment, I feel like you deserve to know that, in fact, many people were interested in knowing how the interviews went. Mostly because I raved about the "amazing opportunity" for two days to anyone who'd listen—before going spontaneously mute on the subject.

Not least of all were my parents, who cornered me after I came back inside from the phone call.

How did it go? Why don't you seem happy? How much did they offer? What happens now?

I fielded formal requests for comment from virtually everyone. A lot of them suspected my career choice was a mistake from the beginning and weren't surprised a magical job fell through at the last minute. They'd never met a private Flight Attendant but there was *no way* they made the kind of money I described. They weren't just cautious—they were convinced I had embroiled myself in some kind of scam.

Coming clean would prove them all right, wouldn't it?

No, I put the thought out of my mind. Maybe this *one* guy used his plane for sex and lies, but what were the chances everyone did?

My other friends were satisfied with, "It wasn't the right fit for me." My parents would not be dissuaded so easily, though. They hounded me for several days, demanding the truth.

"It just seemed like the perfect job."

"You can't be so picky."

"You should really reconsider."

"Do you want to live with us forever?"

"You should at least give it a try, I mean, what's the worst thing that could happen?"

Fine. You asked for it.

"They wanted me to fuck his girlfriends and his pilot!"

Silence.

So did I learn a lesson? Maybe! Something about "not counting chickens before they snatch."

CHAPTER 2

THE INTERLOPER

Hello, Flight Fam. This is your co-captain, James Styron writing now.

This book and these stories are not mine. These perspectives are entirely Danielle's, and the experiences, the trauma she's suffered, it all belongs to her, exclusively.

Well, almost.

See, while Danielle travelled the world with some of the biggest names on the planet, I lived and worked in New York. During this time, I was often on the other end of a frantic phone call hearing about the worst parts of her job. I heard about the people, excesses, the cruel monsters, and the vapid villains.

I learned that being rich and famous is a useful facade for the tyrannical and terrible.

I learned that money and fame don't make people good and decent.

Often, it turns them into exactly the opposite.

Danielle wants her stories to encourage the world to be a better place. Her hope is that you, the reader, might see your worst self in the caricatures within these pages, and be dutifully horrified. She wants to hold up the mirror and inspire us all to be better.

I hope that happens, too, although my faith in humanity is not as strong as hers.

My hope is that we knock the rich and/or famous down from their golden pedestals.

Regular people of Earth, hear me when I say this:

You, as you are—in your state of normalcy, in your daily grinds to survive—bring more value to your lives and to the people you share your lives with than 99.9 percent of the people who fly on private jets. You have stronger beliefs, greater convictions, and more generosity—materially and spiritually—than the ghouls I saw torture my sister for the better part of a decade.

Do not believe that you *are* less because you *have* less. Those who perpetuate that lie have more than they could use in ten lifetimes…and are miserable cunts because of it. As full as their lives are, most of these people are empty inside.

Unfathomable wealth will not—cannot—*make* you happy. It's just a tool. It will amplify whoever or whatever you already are.

Remember that.

CHAPTER 3

OVER-ASSISTED LIVING

I have major respect for assistants. Their jobs are some of the hardest on the planet, as their singular focus is anticipating the needs of another unusually high-functioning human being. It combines forethought, communication, and confidence; it requires getting the shit kicked out of you for other people's mistakes. It ain't pretty.

Many clients depend on multiple assistants. And when I say "depend on" I'm saying "would be useless without."

This client's assistant cluster is hyperactive, always spinning around him in a flurry of lists, food, and phone calls. They share the general sense that, while all are extremely busy, each is equally underutilized—under-appreciated, in their own special way. You catch it in the longing glances, when one gets a pat on the head and the others don't. They feel under-attended and try to make every job the most important in hopes of winning their boss's approval. And, just guessing, their fathers'.

In any case, this is a story about one such assistant.

The client on this flight is, how can I put this delicately…a fuckboy. From somewhere north of the border, he regularly comes to the US to handle business. He speaks English, but occasionally makes calls in French. It's unclear what he does for a living, but it is clear he does a lot of it. Or rather, he does a lot of ordering underlings to do a lot of it, at all hours of the day and night.

Immediately—IMMEDIATELY—upon accepting the trip I am inundated with calls, texts, and frantic emails referencing repeated phone calls and previous text messages; a flurry of sporadic madness that I assume will have run out of steam by the end of the workday.

Oh, no. No no. It's just warming up.

* * *

It goes like this: Every assistant's current goal is their ONLY goal. They're not to breathe, not to speak, not to think—they exist solely to complete the task before them. They live in the hot seat, which means they, themselves, tend to heat up REAL quick. Superman quick. Especially if the last Flight Attendant fucked them over somehow, and the boss took it out on one of the assistants (or, more likely, all of them). It's an "I asked for sushi and steak at 5:00 a.m. so I can eat it fresh at 2:00 p.m.!" kind of dynamic.

Now, on board, in front of me, this particular client is one of THE NICEST, most easygoing clients I've ever worked with. A pleasure in so many ways. They don't shout or snap, or tap their rings on the side of their glass until you make eye contact.

But the assistants, oh man…managing their never-ending lists of demands is as much a process as filling them.

We'll start with the poker set.

"It can't be too light," comes the guidance. "The last one we had was too light. Way too light."

Got it. It needs to be heavy.

"No, not heavy."

Not heavy?

"Not heavy. We had one a few weeks ago that was *too* heavy. So lighter than that one."

I have no idea how much it weighed. I point this out.

"Oh, it was like a standard poker set, but I think they made it out of a heavy material."

Illuminating.

"And the one that was too light, I don't know, it was made out of light stuff."

It's poetry. Don't cry.

This is the most pressing issue at hand. There are two catering orders, a shifting departure time, and an unconfirmed number of guests. Did people click "Maybe" to their invite? Is this the actual Goldilocks of poker decks? Will I get an answer to any of my rhetorical questions?

My first attempt to find this thicc-but-not-too-thicc poker set is a lesson in how to find nothing while frustrating store owners.

I have an out of body experience describing the item to the clerk. "It's a professional poker set, but not the light kind, or the super heavy kind, the normal, regular weight…professional… poker set."

I run out of steam at the end. His expression takes a puzzled position. This is a new question. Does he know how much his poker sets weigh? Can he cover his confusion with confidence?

My uncertainty is spreading. He seems to give up on whatever his plan of attack was and goes with honesty.

"I'll level with you, I don't know what the hell you're talking about."

Beat.

"People like this one." He throws a thumb toward his shoulder, gesturing to a box behind him.

Perfect, can I bludgeon myself with it?

Fantastic.

* * *

While you imagine me running between five—yes, *five*—different specialty game shops, it's a good time to discuss catering. One of the many benefits of flying private is having complete control over what shows up on your plate. You hate arugula? Gone. Craving vegan sushi? Sure thing. You want to stink up the cabin with pickled carp and raw onion? Fuck you, but we can make that happen.

And trust me when I say I've seen it all.

Or I thought I had.

Here's a fun puzzler: If you're making a salad, but you only use lettuce and salt, is it technically a salad? Chew that over while we talk about "guacamole."

It's generally made with avocado, onion, tomato, cilantro, lemon and lime juice, salt and pepper, maybe some garlic and jalapeño if you're feeling frisky. A raw egg (according to my Colombian friend) or a scoop of Fage (if you're a basic bitch who still eats dairy). Chips, plated. It's guacamole.

So says you.

Hang on to your mincer.

Have I mentioned this job is tedious AF? No?

Consider yourself warned, then, because it will introduce you to doctorate level classes in Mundane Shit People Do. Or, more to the point, the shit people ask their assistants to do.

By the time I realize what's happening, it's too late. I have been deputized—so surrogate staff I become.

There is one rule of flying: keep the client happy. Happy clients equal more flights, equal more work, and so on. It's what makes the world go 'round.

So I am actively fielding requests regarding the consistency of the guacamole. Apparently, they're primarily concerned that it will have too many lumps in it.

Yikes. Is that a thing?

Ping.

"There might be too many lumps in the guacamole," the text reads.

"It can't be too lumpy. Can you check that," says another.

Ping.

"Did you buy it from a store?"

Ping.

"Was it smashed by hand? Sometimes they process it in a factory. Make sure it's smashed by hand."

Ping.

"Who made it?"

Probably not Wolfgang fucking Puck?

I offer to make it.

Ping.

"No no, absolutely not, put it through catering."

Ping.

"Are there onions?"

I specifically requested no onions, as specially requested by you, several times. There are no onions.

Ping.

"Very mild. Not spicy at all."

Right.

Ping.

"What about nuts? ARE THERE NUTS IN THE GUACAMOLE?"

Where does this guy get his guacamole? Did I miss an allergy? Does he mean pine nuts? Like sprinkled on the top? I'm flipping furiously through my notes for any mention of a nut allergy.

Ping.

"No allergy. They just hate the sight of nuts."

They hate. The sight. Of nuts.

Okay, mate, I guess that makes two of us. If there's anything els—

Ping. Ping.

Why would I even ask.

"Cilantro? Is this guacamole made with cilantro?"

"LEAD IS MASSIVELY ALLERGIC TO CILANTRO."

Allergic? Massively? It's not even minor-ly mentioned in his file. It's not in any of my notes. I press the assistant.

Ping.

"Well, not actually allergic, but HATES cilantro."

And onion. And jalapeños. And we're *sure* we're still talking about guacamole?

I break the news gently: I believe, yes, there is cilantro in the dish. It is a traditional ingredient. It is, arguably *the* defining ingredient. But unlike the missive on onions, "no cilantro" is a brand new request.

Had I texted over pictures of next week's winning lottery numbers—had I accused him of defrauding his boss—I would have gotten a smaller reaction. The judgement is swift and severe. The assistant makes it clear, despite repeatedly not actually ever making it clear, that "guacamole" in this world is made of three things:

Avocado, lime juice, and salt.

Hold the lumps.

* * *

The quick lil' flight we're full-ass doomsday prepping for is shorter than a Marvel movie. And while I have no idea how he feels about films, I am well versed in his take on music. Intrigued, you say? You didn't.

You will be.

Word came down, at some point, that on one of the previous flights, the client couldn't hear the music as loudly as he wanted to.

To be clear, when a client wants to hear music, they ask the Flight Attendant to turn the music on. It's not always welcome, so the stereo's default position is "off."

His penchant for the greatest artists of the *brain spasm* "'90s Rock Movement" just wasn't being satisfied on his last flight with me. This time we need to scratch that itch. The only sound system that hits the spot for him is a bassy Bose speaker.

I love me a brand-new glossy Bose fresh out of the box. There are both higher end and lower end models, but there's something yummy and modern about their look and the undeniable quality of their sound.

Rather than listening to the assistants suggest we try re-equipping the whole fucking plane, I offer an easier solution: we carry an additional travel speaker on board.

Ping.

"Is it Bose?".

Big 'ol sigh. I have no earthly idea. No lunar clue. I threw it in a cart three months ago when I was Supermarket-Sweeping a Best Buy, two minutes before closing, for another media-minded lunatic.

I check.

Not Bose.

Not acceptable.

So that's why, in literal seven-degree weather, during the sunrise, a few hours before departure, I am slipping on ice in front of the tall skinny door to an electronic store. The friend of a friend who had promised to have the gear raises the security gate in a rush of sound and steel in a single, wince-inducing motion. He's happy to take the money. Less so to be personally brokering the deal.

The shop is hot. The radiators are hissing like a box of Medusas as he disappears behind a wall, flipping light switches on his way. Is there a specific word for hoarders who actually sell their things? Piles of DVD and Blu-ray players, routers, stereo systems, and speaker sets tower into view as the house lights rise.

"Don't touch anything!" he calls from nowhere.

Would not dream of it.

Less than a minute later, the man emerges holding a box in each hand. He sees something on my face, a judgement more than likely. Glancing around the store, he shrugs.

"I do a lot of business online."

Oookay. That tracks. Online is the future, right (wrote the book writers, without a hint of irony)?

He is explaining, in great detail, what will and will not work with the speakers.

There is an App. Have I downloaded the App? He pops the second "P" in a way that, when someone today asks me "What are you thinking about?" it's that. It's usually that.

I haven't downloaded the App.

"Download it before you get on the plane to make sure it works correctly."

Noted.

"And make sure you charge the speakers for at least seven hours first—they got about three hours now, at maybe twenty percent, or thirty-five, maybe forty percent normally, with a one-twenty wall plug for a standard three inch aux cable, if you want."

Umm, what the actual fuck is he saying?

"Eight hours on a full charge, but the 3.2 wireless battery adds an indefinite live span." His monologue on numbers and intro to engineering complete, he pauses.

"Are you gonna want those batteries?"

Anything to make this conversation end.

My takeaway is that I need to figure out how to cram a seven-hour charge into the next ninety minutes. Several thousands of dollars and a hundred years of instruction later, my task finished, I wobble triumphantly onto the ice again.

I'm sliding my way toward what is sure to be *the* best flights the client has ever taken. The "modest" thousand dollar spread of French cheeses and organic charcuterie, the freshest fruits, grilled asparagus, steamed vegetables, freshly baked gluten-free bread, specialty crackers, and yes, caviar, is on its way to the plane.

The other amended catering order has been executed as well, though I would have liked to actually *speak* to the person who ended up making the guacamole…

Oh wait, I can: I cut it from catering and made it myself. Hand smashed, baby.

* * *

So there we are, all headed to meet this "easygoing," "super chill" client for the flight of the century.

I've followed every direction to a T, nailed the speaker set-up like I'm Steve Jobs' IT guy, and we are ready to rock that Dave Matthews, or…I'm guessing something Seattle-ish in flannel? My '90s were TLC, No Doubt, and Missy Elliott. The whole gloomy mic grunge thing missed me.

But let's mosh, nerds!

Mr. Fuckboy finally shows up, several hours later than he scheduled (sarcastic fake shock). AS SOON AS his Ferragamos touch the cabin carpet, I offer to explain our recently updated speaker system, as adjusted to his specifications. I assume the assistant has gotten my messages regarding the App: if they wanted to play DJ, they have to download it and connect via Bluetooth.

It requires a bit of tech savvy but it's not rocket science.

The client's reaction to my multiple lines of instruction drifts from resistant to confused, then swings to annoyed before flipping into full exasperation.

I confirm these were the speakers he wanted.

"Well, yeah. I guess I didn't realize they were so much work. That's annoying."

Errrm. Not as annoying as hunting them down at 7:00 a.m. I have no response. Well, nothing that won't get me fired.

Then he sticks out his hand. It's holding his phone. He's handing his phone to me. But actually.

"Can't *you* just do it?"

It's a phrase that can't be said without sounding pitiful.

I smile. Yes. I handle it.

Between his phone, the buffet, and the poker set, I've been prepping for this flight for daysssss. There's more food than a full plane could eat in three flights. The hand-smashed ingredient-less salt-guac sits ready to serve in the fridge. The perfect poker set awaits, balanced, mid-weight, so perfect and expensive the assistant could have handpicked it. And the music is ready to rock.

I've been practicing my head bangs all week, mostly against walls and the occasional door frame, but it counts.

Wheels up.

And then?

Silence. No song requests.

No one plays poker.

Or touches the "guacamole."

Well-played, Satan.

CHAPTER 4

JUST THE TIP(S)

We're having fun here, right?

Well settle down, because I want to turn a chair backward like a cheugy substitute teacher and get real with y'all for a second.

When I got into this industry I always heard about crazy tips. I heard about the girlies getting cash, jewelry, even cars, as a thank you. I always assumed they'd witnessed a murder or discovered a celebrity was really twenty rats in a human suit. I thought it might be urban legend. I still sort of do.

By the time you get around to eating the sushi platter, those fishies are old enough to get on Medicare. Ditto for your breakfast eggs. Thank God for refrigeration. Y'all will ask for raw fish and wonder why you get bubble guts forty thousand feet in the air.

Knowledge is power, bitches.

I didn't expect to make a trillion dollars serving Diet Cokes and eight-hour old sashimi.

I never thought I'd make a killing doing this job—and for the record, I haven't.

I did, maybe stupidly, expect to be fairly compensated for my work. It's a radical idea, I know. Rich people call it "socialism" and "handouts" when us poor people want decent money for labor. They're staunchly opposed to sharing wealth, even for a job well done; ironically, when their mismanaged businesses start to crumble, (remember the collapsing banks in 2008?) it's often our tax dollars that keep them running. They keep 100 percent of the profits while the public pays their debt. Hypocrisy, thy name is corporate socialism. Nice work if you can get it.

While my job is relatively easy for intuitive caretakers, it's not an easy job. It requires a diverse skill set that few people possess. It's rapid party planning, coordinating, and hosting for groups of total strangers. It's accounting, book keeping, and project managing on the daily. You play chef and server, but if that plane goes down the Flight Attendant is literally deputized to manage the surviving party.

You've got to master the hard skills and have God-like soft skills just to keep your head above water. You need wit, patience, creative problem-solving, and clairvoyance to get through the day. It's a hundred simultaneous jobs.

The people we work for are experts, too: in delegation, scotch-drinking, and being giant pains in our collective ass. For all their middling talent at taking credit for employee accomplishments, our overlords are rewarded with obscene salaries and quarterly bonuses.

We haggle with Accounts Payable over line items on an invoice and fight to get reimbursed for *their clients'* catering orders (more on that later). They call us lazy and entitled for hesitating when requests fall outside of our job duties. *As if* they would perform a service for free. They don't do favors; they receive them.

This is all to say that I never expected to be somebody's do-bitch.

Do-Bitch:

What professional athletes call the unofficially "employed" (a.k.a. paid in cash) who do the shit they don't want to do.

It's assistant work without the job security.

What kind of shit, you ask? Like running to the little bodega to get a pack of Skoal; picking up dry cleaning; watching a dog when they're out of town, or walking said dog when they're too high to do it themselves.

A do-bitch might take out the trash, get a car detailed, pick up drugs—or even test them out like the poor poison-risking, food-tasting bastards who would try the King's food before he'd eat it.

They do the nonsense none of us want to do. They do it (bitch) because they're enthralled with the world of professional athletes. They'll do anything to stay in orbit, like an over-eager moon.

* * *

Becoming a do-bitch certainly wasn't the point of FAA training. A typical plane is about the size of a living room, so it's not difficult for a passenger to get off their ass and walk to the snack basket; when they opt to ask the attendant to do it for them, they're asking her to be a do-bitch. They do it a lot. It's baffling.

She's undoubtedly working on one hundred things which trump this request. Making her hold up a bunch of snacks is quite possibly the dumbest waste of her time. It's not Southwest. We don't generally bring a snack basket around the cabin. If you want *that* specific service, fly commercial. I'm busy plating gourmet meals like I'm Gordon fucking Ramsay.

Still, in my role as caretaker, sometimes I am cast as the do-bitch. Not just with snacks: With kids, with pets, and with any number of other non-Flight Attendant services the clients ask for.

In the moments where I'm going over and above to accommodate the request—again, things the client and/or their offspring could EASILY do themselves, I would start to wonder if I may get tipped for my service. My inner voice bursts out laughing at the notion, much the way I imagine a client would if asked point-blank about tipping. Parting with money is hard enough for them; why pay extra for something a Flight Attendant will do for free?

One of my bosses slapped a couple hundred dollar bills into my palm on a regular basis...more of a bonus than a tip, but I don't want to split hairs. But, it's a rare event to see a client be that generous.

A former client routinely tipped $500 a flight, but that man was ridiculously happy in his life. He also had generational wealth, both of which likely contributed to his unwavering generosity. The typical client believed *not* calling you gutter trash (to your face) was almost better than cash. Money comes and goes—the memory of being treated with basic common courtesy lasts forever.

I had clients who loved to play poker on board. They played with tens of thousands of dollars, sometimes in one hand. Did they turn me into a do-bitch? Absolutely. Did I wait on them hand, foot, and tits with a smile? Of course! Did I keep my mouth shut about the secrets they spilled in front of me? You bet.

And over the hundreds of collective hours we spent together, not one of those fuckers tossed me a dollar for my efforts, my silence, or my exceptional service. NOT ONE TIME did they think to show their appreciation with more than a mumbled thanks. If lewd comments or drunken invitations for sex had value, I'd be on my own private jet right now—but I checked with the banks.

Still worthless.

If you pay for your own flight, it runs upwards of $30K. The prevailing notion might be that it's all-inclusive, which seems like a plausible thought process for the business owners and families that foot their own bill.

The people that really blow my mind are the high profilers: Studios usually pay for the flights because they're on tour, but god*damn*. How are they *so* needy and *so* cheap? It's like, pick a struggle…

They'll fly with ten other people and not a single person pays a dime to be there. The least they could do is break a bitch off a hundred dollars…I meannnnn, you make a bajillion dollars for fuck sake.

Also, tipping goes A LONG WAY to good service. I'm not saying we spit in your food, because I have never heard of a story of that nature on private jets. And trust me, this is the place I'd share if I had.

Buuuut commercial flights? Maybe some First Class Flight Attendants wipe the dinner rolls of massive assholes in toilets—just saying.

I know people are in a full-blown panic these days over tipping culture. It feels like the world has their hand out asking for a little something extra...and people are *not* into it, honey.

But tipping for good service has always been the standard. Plus, fuck the standard. We're talking about a luxury industry here. It's not fucking Denny's. Nothing is standard when it comes to this level of wealth. So it follows that nothing is standard in terms of expectations, in service, or staff.

There are a lot of moving pieces to make your trips to Aspen, St. Barth, and Sardinia flawlessly happen. It's so easy to fuck up a detail and ruin the trip. You'd never know that because it doesn't happen. We're professionals—and we're fucking great at our jobs.

We're at the plane three hours before you even thought about showing up. We work around the clock because you couldn't be bothered to send the catering order to your assistant until midnight last night. We're supposed to make your trip memorable, make your meals Michelin, and take your terrible secrets to the grave. And for what? A $500 flat fee for three days of work?

It's not cheap to live this professional Flight Attendant life. Nails done to perfection every two weeks. Hair done on the regular. Gym memberships to keep us energized and fit enough to carry bags worth fifty times what we make in a year. We spend hundreds of dollars on make-up so we don't look like we just woke up and rolled out of bed—even though we absolutely did. We buy expensive suits and accessories because *we* know *you* know what expensive clothing looks like.

That's what it's like to be a Flight Attendant.

The pilots, meanwhile, jump out of bed thirty minutes before we have to be downstairs. We're lucky they shower their stank off first. They throw on an ill-fitting suit—issued and paid for by the company—slap on some deodorant, and comb the hair they have left. The expenses are minimal but their salaries are high—six, even seven figures.

And they still will remind us that if we get a tip, the proper thing to do is to split it evenly with them.

Also, we didn't get tipped. Stop fucking asking.

While we're on the subject of paying a bitch, let's touch on the yearly salary you assholes think it's okay to pay women for being Flight Attendants. If one more company comes at me with a $60,000 salary to live in NYC, I'm gonna hang up on them. It's incredibly disrespectful to say you pride your entire company on the service we provide, to claim it's what sets your company apart from all the other lame ass charter services and then lowball the shit out of our salaries You didn't even pay for our training, which runs about 5K the first year, and then you throw out a number we can't even live on. Seriously?

Most of us are single ladies, and don't lie, that's exactly what you want. Unattached, no kids, free to be at your beck and call anytime, day or night. Meanwhile, you pay us like we are in double income households and pretend these are good salaries. The cost of living is rising like the heat in the Sahara Desert in July, and you know it because you're generally the ones driving the prices. By the way, we know you give pilots a raise every year, meanwhile one well-known charter company has been paying $550 a day to their contractors for the better part of a DECADE. When your clients own literal airplanes you cannot cry poverty. But, you bet your sweet ass we can because a box of cereal is $9 in the cities you require us to live in.

So seriously, FUCK YOU, PAY US, because if we unionize, you guys are fucked.

CHAPTER 5

POWER TRIP

I used to yearn to fly with women. It's a man's world in aviation, and it's a rare and usually fleeting occasion that you get to fly women who are self-made. Usually, it's their husband's account. You get all their husband's info on the trip sheet and they have one little description at the bottom that says, "is vegan sometimes." So annoying, to say the least. I mean, she's your wife, she should be more than an afterthought. Someone should be keeping tabs on her as equally as they are on their husbands. They both fly on the fucking plane, for Christ's sake. But, alas, usually these high-functioning CEO's care more about themselves and their preferences...shocker.

So you can imagine my excitement to get a plane full of women. I am pumped! I get even MORE pumped when their riders consist of nothing extra, as they sometimes bring their own catering and only request the standard onboard snacks.

Rider (raɪ-dər):

A list of requirements, requests or conditions that a client expects onboard for their pleasure and enjoyment.

SCORE! Major score! Basically, in those cases, I have to show up, be nice, and pour lots of Diet Coke. BOOM. My specialty, smiling and pouring diet beverages. Let's gooooooo!

This story is not one of those stories.

This story is about a group of women who make no fucking sense.

These ladies roll up with an ungodly amount of luggage. No surprise there. Most of the women I fly pack like they're going to Paris Fashion Week. Sustainable fashion is in, you consumeristic hoarders. God forbid you recycle a look.

As the pilot is giving his brief, explaining that he knows how much they fly and they don't necessarily need the brief, but he is blah blah bound by the rules of the blah blah operation they are flying on blah blah. The middle one gets this look in her eyes. Why? Literally, no one knows. Straight fuck-you eyeballs. Staring fireballs directly into his eyes as he talks and continues to explain there is no smoking in the lav, it is a felony to do so, and so on. He nervously continues.

As he drones on, she grabs at the snack basket like a hawk snatching at a squirrel running in the brush, her glossy, manicured talons scratching at anything she can grab that is in a foiled bag. By now, she's found her target. He is wrapping up his speech. She is still dead-eyeing this mofo. He looks even more nervous, unsure of what is happening. She looks dead on the inside. She opens the perfect snack bag full of crispy chips, maybe it was Pringle's, who can say at this point. The drama is palpable. She peels open the bag slowly, deliberately. She reaches out, the bag in hand, over the isle, and dumps it upside down onto the carpet.

IN FRONT OF THE PILOT.

He looks at her, looks at the chips on the floor, confused as fuck by the shitty power play this bitch has created, and she politely thanks him for the brief.

WHAAAAAAT IN THE ACTUAL FUCK.

Completely bewildered, he turns around and heads back to the cockpit. He does not clean up the circus of chips that have been dumped onto the floor by this Karentown character. He does not scold her. He does not ask her to clean those babies up. Basically, he completely ignores it and taxies for take-off.

These ladies fly all the time. It's part of their job—going here, there, and everywhere promoting anything anyone will pay them a dollar for. They know better. She chose violence.

As it turns out, none of the chicks have any class because no one picked up anything off the carpet and were perfectly happy walking over greasy, crunchy chips for the entirety of their flight. So much so that they were ground into the carpet and a cleaning crew had to be dispatched to the plane to clean up the hundreds of tiny pieces.

CHAPTER 6

THE CLEANSE

When you do a job like this long enough you become intimately familiar with certain clients. If you fly them enough, you're basically guaranteed to see all of their emotional states. Often, these emotional states feature Anger and Impatience, but that's nearly guaranteed in the event that a client is dieting or—God save us—fasting. They often drift between the two.

But really, it's the juice cleanse you have to watch out for.

Oh, the juice cleanse. A favorite among the elite, the super skinny, and the "healthy sugar" addicted. You've probably done one or know someone who won't stop talking about theirs.

I will preface this story by saying, personally, I love a good juice cleanse. We're talking kale, cucumbers, and—not a joke—literal pounds of celery.

I can make it several days, but it's tricky. By the end of day three, while my mind is clearer and I feel trimmer, slimmer, and fully detoxified, I'm useless. I can't cleanse if I've got shit to do. I don't have the energy or the patience. And my homemade juicing extravaganza leaves out the ten pounds of sugar you drink in the pre-bottled ones. They say sugar is more addictive than cocaine...I think it makes us act crazier, too.

* * *

While I am not *your* personal assistant, I will do my absolute best to accommodate your needs with appropriate notice. If you fail to provide notice, I can guarantee nothing, not one damn thing. BUT, being the bomb ass Flight Attendant I so casually *am*, I always have gluten-free, vegetarian, and vegan options onboard. You're welcome.

Some background is probably useful here. Private trips to Las Vegas happen all the time. You would be shocked—look at me, SHOCKED—to know how many people will pay a king's ransom for a forty-five minute flight. It's...I can't...moving on.

My point is, we know the routine. Client lands. Client goes nuts. One to four days later, client pours whatever's left of their previous selves back onto the jet, and everyone takes the world's most expensive flying nap.

And while the principle is out doing his or her thing—a.k.a. slots and shots—the crews have been known to do a thing or two of their own. Flight Crews have a reputation for being a work hard, play hard bunch, and private flight crews are not exempt. Flight Attendants party, but pilots are a whole different situation. I once saw a pilot fall asleep, sitting bolt upright at the bar, with his hand wrapped around his pint.

As a matter of policy, I don't go hard on school nights. If we're flying the next day, you won't ever find me at the hotel bar having a cocktail before lights out. I can't speak for the industry standard.

On this rare trip, the flight crew is both fun *and* young. "Fun young crew," for the record, is the oxymoron of the century. In my experience, there are only a handful of "fun young pilots" in private aviation, whose vision of a great night extends beyond getting shmammered at the bar and hitting on waitresses. As the Flight Attendant, you're low-key the cruise director of your crew. You are the entertainment. The more fun you are with pilots after hours, the more likely they are to book you on future trips. And no, I don't mean between the sheets; I mean at the obligatory post-flight dinner and drinks.

They're kind of like your dad's friends: a bit nosey, a bit gawky, but generally well-meaning. Just bored. And super inclusive.

But this pilot was none of those things. He was hot, *and* helpful, *and* friendly, and most importantly, hitting on me. Which means my rules about drinking on a school night flew out the Aria window.

He wanted to go *out* out. How could I say no?

So we went out. We had a drink that turned into several drinks that turned into several bars. Bars turned into clubbing at Hyde, and night turned into morning. I'm not entirely sure what time we ended up face down, fully clothed in our separate hotel rooms.

My last vivid memory is of the bartender telling us we finished the Clase Azul, and suggesting that if we wanted to keep sloppily making out we do it anywhere but there.

The next thing I remember is some juice jerk sending word that their *very* special juices for a *very* specific juice cleanse are being requested at the last minute. And could I please just take care of that. The forwarded request came through the pilot from the night before.

How was he functioning? How was he fucking *texting*?

Ugh.

Uggghhhhh.

I need coffee. I need...like...what is it called...food...a snack...some eating kind of something? Breakfast? Is that the answer? A burger?

In my state, one blurry eyeball was able to see this request through a shaking water glass, which it seemed I'd filled from the tap, mind you. Even last night, I knew to avoid those goddamn ten-dollar water bottles. Thank goodness for gorgeous filtered water straight from the tap. Thank you luxury hotels. Our per diem barely covers meals in our exotic locations, let alone the overpriced, artisanal bottles of imported glacier runoff from eons ago.

Like I need a million-year-old parasite.

Ping. The pilot is relentless.

"Are you going?"

I moan. Audibly.

Ping.

"It's under the alias, just remember."

An alias. For the assistant.

No. One. Knows. Who. You. Are.

It's always the bloody assistant. And guys think their girlfriends are high maintenance.

Ping.

"Do you want me to go?"

Yep. I do. I really, reallllly want him to go. If he gets the juice now, I'll fly the plane later. Even Steven.

Ping.

"I'm super hungover."

Agreed.

Ping.

"Last night was fun."

Ohhh my shit. What happened?

Ping.

"I was thinking about you this morning."

Stop. Noooooo ssttoopppp.

Did I totally forget we sucked on each other's faces in front of literally the entire fucking bar for who knows how long? OMG am I about to have to walk these lips through the entire casino, past the scene of the grime?

Wow.

What a way to wake up.

* * *

I sip a Nespresso and wait for the caffeine to kick in, massaging my temples.

Last night *was* fun, though. Too many shots. Way too many… tongues? Yes. Like waaaaaaay too many. Ugh. I gag. The making-out-like-the-actual-plane-was-going-down was fun, too. I laugh because I can't believe there is actually a fun, hot, young pilot. He's a unicorn. I gag again, not sure if that is the hangover or the shame.

Yawn. This one might be a throw-up, actually.

I collect myself, get dressed, and stagger into the elevator. Sweating, I stroll into the lobby of this very swanky, very loud hotel, I immediately realize I should have kept my earplugs in.

I make it to the very specific juice cleanse operation and manage to order myself a proper green juice to whip my brain into shape, before requesting my *Gulliver's Travels* juice order.

"We packed them in coolers for you. We thought it'd be easier for you to carry."

"Cooler" is an overstatement. The bottles were packed in what is the equivalent of a Whole Foods bag lined with tin foil.

It's made of the same thick polyester your awkward aunt calls her "chillax clothes": Almost strong enough to build shelter out of, but not so strong you'd trust it.

You know the ones. They have handles and a zipper, and the thinnest layer of insulation modern industry has produced. They try to hide it under heavy branding and crowd-sourced artwork, but a shitty bag's a shitty bag.

It's not a cooler. At best, it's a coolish, you fruit pusher.

I stare at the bags. The Juice Queen beams a blinding smile, extending her arm and hand with a piece of paper dangling off of it: the inventory.

Convenient.

I'm reading it. We've got your standard reds and greens, your pineapples and orange juices (for the lightweights), aaand…is it nut juice? We're juicing nuts? Now you've got my attention. I guess if a nut can be milked it can be sucked through a processor. Wow, "nuts, 'juiced' and 'sucked'"? There's a joke in there somewhere (you can @ me when you find it).

So it's dawning on me, in this legume-y moment of discovery, that I have no actual place to store this cache of juice. Until I have access to the plane or get to the airport, these bottled bastards are ticking time bombs. Queue action track.

I heave them off the counter—and collapse directly to the floor. I can hear the circular sound of something heavy rolling away. I've also discovered my new saddle bags contain approximately sixty-five pounds of glass and a thousand pounds of liquid.

And just coming back to nut juice: I still don't understand. How many pounds of pressure do you think it takes to juice a nut? Is this like that "blood from a stone" bible-y thing, or like a science-y, laboratory diamond thing? How much juice do you get from one nut? Do you need a bushel for one whole juice? How many trees are in this bag?

So. Many. Questions.

Anyway, ole Jenny Juicer is like, "Oh!" in a way that sounds pained and patronizing, but I must have seemed okay because she doesn't actually move. As I struggle to my feet, someone hands me the rogue juice. Not surprisingly, it's a nut juice that tried to make a break for freedom.

Not so fast, ten thousand nuts.

I manage to army crawl the fifteen miles back to my hotel where I see the concierge waving at me. He is thrilled to see that I'm safely back on the premises alive, albeit still grossly hungover.

He grabs the coolers from my arms.

"Holy crap, these are heavy."

Preach it. In reality, it's been about sixteen minutes since I picked up the juices. We need to move. I ask if he'd let me use the industrial fridges.

He hesitates. He's talking about liability, blah, blah, blah. Whatever, I'm not actually asking. We're doing it.

I promise that in the unlikely chance that anyone gets sick off of the nut juice, we will absolutely not call them and complain, or try to hold them accountable, knowing full well that this assistant absolutely, totally would.

Thankfully, that did not happen. But at this point, even if this entourage did get sick off of them, I borderline didn't care. They were all so hungover, they wouldn't blame the juice; this group is bound to drink these things in the first ten minutes then fall asleep. Nap juice. This up front labor might be worth it, I reason.

It's baffling. The client has more money than God; why not have the juice delivered directly to the plane? Those trucks are climate controlled. The order would be juiced fresher, and packaged better...guys, even writing this now, my eyes are rolling so far back into my head I might go permanently blind.

Juices stored, I make it back to my hotel room and am able to pass out again for a couple of hours before this evening's flight. Thank God it's an evening one. The pilot calls to make sure I'm not dead, that I got the juices, and does he need to send me a piece of toast? Hell yes to the toast and if he could put avocado on it before sending it over, I will never ask him for anything in my stupid life again.

* * *

We, (the Crew) assemble and arrive at the plane. Two thirds of us still smell of tequila; one third of us is singularly on his game. The other pilot (who I witnessed *Weekend at Bernie's* himself through the hotel lobby) is slumped against the window. Our hero is sitting with perfect posture, chatting quietly to me and the semi-dead pilot. Neither of us has much to say. Every bump on the road pushes toast the wrong way, up my throat.

Inside every plane is a different galley (a.k.a. kitchen) set up. Smaller designs use a single ice box. The Vegas demigods were smiling on me, because this plane had two. Shoulda played craps (wait, did I play craps?).

Less luckily, the ice boxes already have a full roster. It's where soda, beers, white white (and often red), milk, cream, water, juices, and sports drinks sit when they're not being poured into your cup. Does that seem obvious? It should. There are ten people on the plane, and one man has enough nut punch to fill a pool. I fit maybe two bottles in an ice box—but the inn is full.

It now becomes my job to quickly find a way to store a grocery isle's worth of warming juices without sacrificing literally every other drink on the plane. The client isn't on site yet, so it's not a dire situation. But, internally, I'm not doing great. The stress is rising. And worst, last night's barrel of Clase Azul is making me forget how to improvise.

Oh God, I forgot we finished the bottle at the bar mid-snogfest.

I look around.

I got nothinggg to put these juices in.

Well, I reason, the juice girl called them coolers. I'll put bags of ice in them and they can sort of be stored discretely. It'll have to do for now. Again, it's a quick flight. And they'll drink at least ten, if everyone has one.

Someone from the client's party is on board; I feel them watching me. I stand up and welcome them—and would they like a juice?

"No, that's not for me. [REDACTED] bought that to take home with him."

Oh. My. God.

That's why there are *so* many.

Turns out, this particular man has been on a juice cleanse for God only knows how many excruciating weeks and neglected to inform the staff on the airplane. Rule numero uno, ESPECIALLY as an assistant...inform your jet broker of ALL special dietary needs so that the crew may prepare adequately for your trip.

Suffice it to say, that did not happen.

Also super fun, I learned they do not see me as someone whose job it is to rescue their bodies from the wreckage of a plane crash and keep the survivors alive on rotisserie lizard and rain run-off until we can all be saved. In *their* eyes, I am simply here to mule bag a hundred pounds of cold pressed nut droplets across state lines. I am the assistant's assistant. How may I serve?

"Actually, can I get a Diet Coke?"

Cool.

Super cool.

A few minutes later, the assistant is ready for his first juice.

"I'm taking them all home with me, it's great," he says. He is visibly proud.

I smile. *So* great.

About fifteen minutes into the flight, I notice something shiny in the floor. Weird. No, not shiny—wet. And mobile. I wouldn't call it "gushing." It was more like those scenes where there's a fire and a gas leak, and a little dribble of gas is snaking toward the blaze, while the main character is tied up somewhere nearby. They can only watch.

This is not gasoline. This is water. I can see its origin… those goddamn coolers of juice.

Oh my God, we're going to drown on a plane three miles above the ground. More water, more running fucking water. Now the assistant's giant head is popping up over a seat.

He's all, "Hey, what's that? What's going on?" We're taking on water, you selfish prick, stay in your lane and your seat, I'm dealing with some homeless-ass juices over here. You cannot help me. You caused all of this.

"Just a bit of water," I grin instead.

But wait. My neurons fire. Yes: I have an idea.

I remember we have, essentially, a large steel locker on board. In case of fire, it will keep the flames and embers contained, prevent it from spreading throughout the galley, causing major damage and/or potential fatalities.

It's one of the largest storage compartments on the plane, probably made from the same insulating space metal that gets astronauts through the atmosphere. It's tall, easily accessible, and self-contained. This could work, I think.

There's a catch, and it's less than ideal: The space in question is *technically* a trash can.

I know what you're thinking (so stop it) but hear me out: These planes are kept pretty clean, for the most part. Trash is not tossed into these metal boxes without a bag inside. Industrial trash bags, as in, no actual garbage will usually touch the inside of one of these things.

On top of that, there's virtually no food on board, outside of single-serving chips, Pirates Booty, and protein bars. The "trash" is recycling. This isn't some boozy, piss-soaked New York public trash can or the one in your hoarder friend's scary house. It's clean. It's pristine.

This is happening.

I zip the bags of juice shut, wrestle them into the locker, and set the *almost empty* trash bag on top. And for the forty-five minutes we'd be airborne, I assume the actual saving of his nuts was more important than how it happens.

I am exactly right on another count, too. The clients are as hungover as they could be, so they are only guzzling water, Gatorade, and packages of dry roasted nuts (protein, brah). There's really no "garbage."

At this point, I'm a genius. I must be Sheryl Sandberg because I am leaning the fuck in over here today (and I'm only functioning at like mayyyybe 1 percent).

Everyone is sleeping again. No one saw a damn thing. I win. I deserve a raise. I deserve a medal. I deserve a nap.

I could not have been more wrong.

I could not have underestimated the devastating impact of my genius any less.

The assistant is ready for another juice. The sight of water made him thirsty (Have three, please!) but dude can no longer see the cooler and he's concerned.

"Um, where's the cooler?" he asks with a suspicious dip in the middle of the question.

Ummmmmm, fuck.

I explain very calmly and very quickly and in the lowest voice that has ever come out of my loud ass mouth, that I was forced to move it because of the leakage, sir. The cooler was leaking in the cabin, sir, if you noticed (you did). Lots of sir's being used in this interaction.

"Well where'd you move it to?" This is both a demand and an accusation. He's standing. He wants to see.

Fuck meeeeeee, can a bitch catch a break?!

He follows me to the galley and watches intensely as I open the trash bin. I remove the very light, almost empty trash bag, and reveal their new home. I pull out a juice, holding it up, hopeful.

His eyes get big. My smile gets bigger, as I try to counterweight the expressions forming on his face with my pearly whites. Is it working?

"WHAT THE FUCK?!" he bellows.

It is not working.

I swear he flew up into the air, mouth wide open, limbs flailing, screaming at the top of his lungs.

"What the fuck are you doing?? That is *so* disgusting! I had no fucking idea you were this disgusting. Oh my God, what the fuck, what were you thinking? You are fucking disgusting!"

And on, and on, and on.

We take a lot of abuse in this industry. We go above and beyond to make sure you enjoy your flight. But to be clear, this type of behavior is not tolerated. And I am done tolerating.

The rage coming out of this grown man's face wakes up everyone on the plane. I breathe, wondering if he is about to get physical, and I swear I could still taste tequila.

In that moment, I lost all my fucks.

Besides, you don't shrink when facing down a bear.

I stand up straight and loudly respond that there are ten people on this plane and his selfish ass decided he needed to fill the plane up with the same juices he could have gotten much easier in LA. Instead, he decided to make it my problem on a plane with an ice box the size of one of his shoes.

As wild animals are when frightened by a more powerful force, he visibly recoils, taken aback by the realest talk he's heard since the Wendy Williams show.

He looks almost emasculated as he heads back to his seat with a fresh nut juice. I tell him I'll remove the rest from the bin, dry them, and store them back in the cooler. I also point out that I can't be held responsible in the event that the juices spoil.

He nods, mumbles "oh, that's okay, thank you," still obviously stinging from my rebuke.

Is there a moral?

Maybe, "if you're a huge dick, juice your nuts at home..."

Yeah, that feels right.

CHAPTER 7

THE FULL HEISMAN

I'll level with you: I'm not a huge fan of sports. Ironic considering my first love was a professional athlete. Growing up, I played basketball and volleyball, but I sensed something inherently unappealing about a bunch of kids who possess no fear running full-speed at the same object.

On top of soccer or softball (allegedly "non-contact sports," but a description I violently reject) my school district had plenty of hard-hitting options that were supposed to "build character." It's strange to me that so many parents thought (and probably still think) that letting their kid get the shit kicked out of them in a public arena is actually good for them. I mean, I'm all about overcoming obstacles, but I remember a lot of kids who were forced to play sports, fully against their will.

So, did my parents not love me enough to force me to get black eyes and broken teeth, like so many of the sporty kids in my grade? Was I instinctively repelled by the idea of getting my lights knocked out by some spry bag of hormones set loose on a spray-painted field? Maybe I threatened to run away. It's hard to remember.

My dad took me to a few sporting events when I was a child. I'm not sure it did a whole lot to change my mind (it did not change my mind even slightly). As an adult, my favorite sports team is no team, because I honestly could not give a shit. Have you *met* crazy sports fans? Nooo thank you; there are more important things to get riled up over.

In some ways, though, it is like I play on a major sports team. My job entails a ton of travel, regular training, and, considering the caliber requested for private aviation versus commercial, we are the best in our industry. The MLB of the FAA.

If the crew are the players making stuff happen and driving the event, then the clients are the team owners. They think they know how the game works but they've never played a day in their lives.

Their advice is generally unhelpful, and they themselves are out of touch. Still, they've got a plan, and you're not following it. That's how Flight Attendants end up as free agents.

Huh, so I *can* make sports metaphors.

One of these client coaches has a real hard-on for heckling staff, strangers, and the husband she stole. She's one of those salt-of-the-earth "two-for's," as in she's both a mean-spirited harpy *and* an armchair dictator with a savior complex. Her "projects" are worth everything to her—the staff who make them happen? Let's say they're worth decidedly less.

Some of those people work for her dogs. Not like *for*, but... wait, no. I stand by that. If you're hired on a full-time basis to serve a dog, you work for that dog. It's like being a service dog. But for a dog.

Three dogs. Four assistants. Several other staff members. The client and her family. You can't be *Richie Rich* rich and be expected to take care of your own animals. Or your own needs. Or your own business. That's why folks want big money in the first place: to pay other, poorer people to do the menial labor of life.

Maybe you've heard of it, it's called Capitalism?

That was just a little joke.

The part before (and the part that comes next) is not.

* * *

The dynamic on board is…in a word, toxic. If a happy house buzzes along like a beehive, this hive is perpetually in the throes of Colony Collapse Disorder. Not to worry. It's nothing a little fascist fist pounding can't scare back in line, which is often the way she spoke—on phone calls, while emailing, or using her black eyes to peek into the soul of anyone dumb enough to make eye contact.

This collapsing colony has beautiful homes scattered around the globe like a tiny international empire. Who even knows how they made their wealth? Like every good jet owner, they dabble in multiple businesses.

Diversified revenue streams, darlings.

Everywhere they go they bring this giant shedding, horse-looking, wildebeest dog pack with them. It's sweet, right?

Don't be deceived.

It'd be a whole lot sweeter if this lil' Elm Street nightmare family didn't suck up all the air out of the room, or speak to their staff with half the respect they addressed the aforementioned wildebeests.

But we should be so lucky.

Obviously, this family doesn't actually take care of the dogs. That's why they have staff. There's not *not* a theme emerging here; let's see if you can spot it. (Hint: Money often makes you useless.)

This family travels with several handlers. One per dog, and possibly another thrown in for fun. A handler for the handlers? Makes sense, I guess.

These poor handlers. Their jobs are hanging with pups, I mean, who *else* should be having the most fun with the least amount of work? You are salaried dog entertainment. You're like a manager, but all your clients want are walks, treats, and scratches (good boys).

But it's not all puppy kisses and nap time. The other side of the job seems to be getting straight tortured by their employers.

This couple does everything together—look at me—every-thing.

The man seems nice enough, but I swear his wife is about to have a house drop on her. Maybe she already did. Maybe that's why she's such a monument to misery for every waking moment of her insanely glamorous (but still obviously unfulfilling) life.

I always thought money...man...like real, big, chauffeur my Rolls money—THAT would solve a lotta shit. And it *would*.

Quite frankly, it *does*. Routinely.

These uber-wealthy families don't have to worry about any of the normal bullshit the rest of us worry about. Their landlord isn't raising their rent—they own the building. They have zero idea how their water bill gets paid or how much HOA fees are. I know many women in that world who haven't been into a grocery store in over thirty years. Read that again...*many*, as in, more than a hot yoga class's worth.

Every aspect of these people's lives is managed so that they skip the normal nonsense the rest of the world has to put up with. They've generally never encountered a problem they couldn't swipe their way out of, so it's no wonder so many spouses are driven to create problems for solving.

It's something to pass the time.

So often, the rich and powerful (R&P) have NO chill. Frankie might say relax, but some couples don't know what the *fuck* that means, okay? And they don't have the time to learn.

And also...*fire Frankie.*

This would be one such couple. Textbook R&P, level ten narcissists. She is a former fitness guru, a gorgeous, laser-cut flower (now retired) who helped housewives lose their lady lumps so their fickle husbands wouldn't dump them.

He is a man of—who even fucking knows what he does. He's like every other shady-ass businessman who pops up on a chartered trip. He's soldered to his laptop, firing off emails and speed-reading the *Wall Street Journal*...between looking at young hotties on Snapchat.

The irony of spending your life helping women save their marriages only to be shut out of your own...I mean it's no wonder this lady lives to eviscerate people.

Anyway, one of the unlucky dog handlers on this specific trip was an *extremely* nervous flier. Shit was about to get a whole lot unluckier for him, too. A little gossipy pilot bird told me the handler did not want to take the trip in the first place. He'd apparently done everything in his power to get replaced.

But, there he was before takeoff, drained of all color, pools of sweat forming on his chest like he was midway through a cardio class. He was in real, physical agony, possibly the most nervous flier I've seen to date. Somewhere between a flop sweat and a nervous breakdown. But it's time to take off. So I take my own seat.

After we level out, I return from the cockpit to check on the handler. There I see him…now face down on the cabin floor we have been walking on for two hours (gross). He's whiter than before, somehow. So white. He's Casper the friendly ghost white.

His sweatiness is about to become a danger to the other passengers. His Hoover Dam has burst—all over his face and shirt, and in a shallow swamp of heat and panic beneath him. We may all need to put on lifejackets in case he floods us out.

Before I saw *him*, I could hear *her*. She was *not* offering reassurance.

Fortunately, for Mr. Nausea we only have a three-hour flight. Unfortunately for him, about 89 percent of it is going to be what the pilots described as "aggressively turbulent."

Yikes.

"You should have taken more Dramamine," the client's wife is yelling through the cabin.

Ugh, I cringe. My therapist says "should" is a judgment word. People should-ing all over each other is a red flag; those who always know what's best for you have control issues.

I know, hot take.

"He took some in the car, Mrs…"

All the staff call her Mrs.—myself included.

"Well…he should take more. He obviously didn't take enough," she scoffs. "I mean he's a *grown man*, *clearly* he should have taken more. It's too late now," she trails off after her tirade, sounding irritated and out of ideas.

Ugh, "should" AGAIN. What is *enough* dramamine anyway? How about, maybe you could have just not brought him? He warned everyone several times that something like this would happen. Mrs. either didn't believe him, or didn't care.

In my experience, it's usually the latter. You don't get to be this wealthy by having a ton of empathy.

At this point, I've offered everything from ginger ale to more Dramamine to herbal teas to cold water to homeopathic anti-nausea pills and essential oils—anything I can think of to help him. He can't even speak to decline the help, he just presses his face into the dog. My heart goes out to this guy.

Fortunately, the Mrs. doesn't eat while flying, which means neither can any staff or her husband, so there's no ordered catering on this flight. This is good because at this moment, both our canine and human guests are getting tossed around like a package in the hands of an angry FedEx driver.

The dog handler has become translucent at this point. And there's a chance he's crying a little. Apparently, the thought never even occurred to the Mrs. to just…not…bring him…? And maybe just, and I know this idea is borderline certifiable, but do with one less dog handler? We've already established there are three other proper dog handlers and *at least* two other nannies on board. I'm pretty sure one of them would have been more than happy to save this dude the trauma of being forty-five thousand feet in the air, sweating his wig off, and fighting back projectile vomit all afternoon.

As I look back through the cabin, the handler is now legitimately clinging onto the dog for moral support and lamaze breathing like his life depends on it, because, well, it kind of does. If this dude pukes, like I swear it looks like he's going to, his job is *over*, honey. The only respect he's getting is from the dog, and even that's waning as the turbulence is intensifying. We now have jet-propelled horse-dogs launching themselves into the air, taking full advantage of the reduced gravitational conditions.

Meanwhile, I'm still trying to do my job. I am Gene fucking Kelly in a mine field. I am dodging puppies like Britney Spears dodging laser grids in the "Toxic" video.

Spin, duck, roll, check the wig.

I am glad to be in flat shoes. Don't believe the movies: Any Flight Attendant worth their truffle salt will tell you it's flats twenty-four seven while on client's very expensive carpets. It's for moments exactly like this. And so you don't snag their overpriced specialty carpet with your snaggled TJ Maxx heel. And I thank my pedicured GODDESS for my no-heels policy. I could be army crawling my sprained ankles down the aisle at the base of a puppy pyramid.

As I move from the back of the cabin up toward the galley at the front of the plane, I take note of the "special" dog. Did I mention that one dog is not subject to the rules of the others? It's the one with the terrorized handler. He's got *the* special dog.

I'm not sure why, specifically, this one enjoys an elevated status...it's a little like ranking your children, which, ugh, don't get me started. Maybe she thinks pitting them against one another will make them stronger. Who knows? Fucking rich bitches.

This dog and attached handler have scooted to the front of the plane and are jostling around by the cockpit. The other dogs have successfully freed themselves from their handlers.

The canines are now running a circuit—floor to chair to mid-air launch, two seconds of weightlessness, repeat. I am dodging flying fur bodies and frantic handlers as I tip tap closer and closer to the special one.

Now, this special dog is shaggy AF. Maybe that's why he's so special? Maybe he's a former hair farm for an '80s rock band.

He's some kind of German Shepard/Cousin Itt hybrid. Mrs. is warning me not to step on her dogs.

Duh, lady!

"You *cannot* step on him, okay? Be careful. *Can. Not.*"

As I carefully plant one twinkle-towed foot after another, I make it past the Mrs. without another barking order. But I can feel her eyes boring holes into my legs. She's the Russian gymnastics judge: I'm definitely losing points. It's all over her face. Another foot plants. Nice. I shift my weight—just as the plane tosses us again. I manage not to move either foot and stay rooted to the spot.

I'm nailing this.

Or so I thought.

I feel the boniest ghost hand wrap around my arm. It's powered by the force of a thousand Grim Reaper claws. It's an eagle with a manicure. It's a sentient grappling hook.

It's the Mrs.

I'm moving in slow motion, moving toward her. Oh, no, wait—I'm moving away from her. I'm flying, soaring like the bird whose claw propelled me. For a few seconds, I've joined the dogs on their circuit. I get a rush, being airborne inside of a plane. It is exhilarating.

Until I crash directly into the bulkhead. Not to worry, my head breaks my fall.

I quite literally pick myself up off the floor and turn to face my assailant. She is still there, arm outstretched like a seated Heisman trophy. She must have read "What in the hell" all over my face, because Mrs. Claws starts a full-throated justification of what she'd done.

"You were *way* too close to him, he's a *rescue*! You need to be more careful where you step so *I* don't *have* to push you! He's very, *very* sensitive."

Girl what?!

She's saying more things but my ears are ringing, and I haven't quite caught my balance yet. The takeaway is I deserved to be pushed, it was my fault, and hopefully I'd learned my lesson.

Here's the real lesson:

IT IS A **FELONY** TO ASSAULT FLIGHT CREW.

In the event you manhandle one of us, the FAA will manhandle you directly to the FBI. If convicted, you may be placed on the no-fly list, and face the possibility of fines and jail time.

Keep your talons to yourselves, people.

CHAPTER 8

FILTHY FLIERS

Bet you didn't know that cleaning crews usually only deep clean jets once they're back at home base. Yep. So while you're partying it up in Miami this weekend, your Flight Attendant only has a lil' ole Lysol wipe to "clean" the bathroom. That's after you and all your buddies blew it up from that eight-plus hour old sashimi you insisted on ordering for the flight down.

Yeah, we think it's gnarly too: The same hands that serve you food are also wiping down the lav. Light cleaning is just part of the job. And don't worry, we do use gloves, but other than a Lysol wipe, all we have is an FAA approved spray for the rest of the cabin. And it's not one of those hospital-grade type sprays that kills every ungodly thing that could be lurking on the various surfaces you touch and the tables you eat on. There's also a chance that the microfiber towel we use was used yesterday, too. There's only ever a few on board. Blame it on shrinkflation.

What if one of your kids gets on that steel bird with a staph infection? Oh, we're all going down. Any one of us who has an opening in their skin is subject to contracting the infection.

Planes are usually on cleaning schedules. Meaning it's likely those babies won't be cleaned until the end of the month.

Here's why: When a plane goes back to its home base, that's where it's thoroughly cleaned and detailed. It's sort of like when Minute Maids comes to your house. They really get in there, hitting all the places you don't think about. They deep-clean. Your place probably looks brand new and smells *awesome* when they leave, right? Right.

Now, what about when *you* clean your scummy lil' house? Sure, you may have binged CleanTok. Sure, you "learned" how to properly clean. But when a professional does it, everything is sparkling and the job is just a million times better. Everyone knows that's just science.

It's also worth pointing out that the billion-dollar industry is pretty anti-spending-money-on-anything. The main reason owners have thought it was totally acceptable to spend two hours a month (if that) deep-cleaning their jets is because Flight Attendants are drafted into janitorial work.

So, try not to think about those Kith Kids whose sticky fingers were all over the buttons just a few hours before you boarded. Or the spoiled, shedding Golden Retriever that was licking the window you are thoughtfully posing in front of. It's totally fine, because we wiped it down, definitely. We definitely did not forget to wipe it down...*checks notes*... definitely.

So, this is really a PSA: Stop being dirty birdies on flights. Because our primary job is your safety. It's making sure you are not in danger, and that if said danger pops up, we work with your pilots to ensure everything is handled to the best of our capabilities. Your job is to not be a gross human.

CHAPTER 9

THE NEVER-ENDING STORY

Oh boy. This guy. Does not. Stop. TALKING.

Ohhh, the patience she is exuding. The ethereal, beautiful, captivating, ethereal (I said it twice because it's double what you're imagining), Goddess-esque Buddha-meets-Deepak-Chopra-in-a-zen-garden level patience she's showing him as he embarks on his fourth consecutive hour of babbling about his sad, depressing, traumatic life.

His life sounds very hard, very full of obstacles, and very full of parents. It sounds lonely and, frankly, just plain sad. It also sounds like he's confused his worldwide icon/girlfriend with a family therapist that's paid to listen to his sad, tragic, long, sad (yes, we said sad twice) tale. He must have mistaken the private jet for a private office adorned with Psychology degrees and Rorschach-inspired, Jackson Pollockey wall art, in which he'd be free to confess his deepest fears and acute loneliness.

He is emotionally vomiting everywhere—and all of his mommy and daddy issues are landing on his girlfriend, along with a bit of spittle. Ironically—age-wise—she *could* have been his mommy.

Meanwhile, I am seriously awed by this diva's patience. It's otherworldly. Like, potentially, specifically, from the pharmaceutical world, but I'm not a doctor. I'm more of a bitchy, judgmental, non-certified therapist and life coach, but even I know glassy eyes when I see them. Plus, she seems content to let this dude drone on and on. That leaves us two options: 1) She's a classically trained monk, or 2) There's a party in her tummy to which several friends RSVP'd. Xanax, and/or maybe Valium. I'm guessing they each had a plus one to the event, too.

OMFG he's been monologuing for three days and we're not even to the Rockies yet. Time has ceased to mean anything. We're outside the laws of the universe. What the *actual*, liminal fuck.

She turns her head toward me and gives the signal. I smile and nod, obediently approaching to refill her glass of red wine.

The two constants in this vacuum are a male voice and its wheelbarrow full of trauma. Nothing else is real. We're trapped with it, like a kidnapping without the Stockholm Syndrome. His hostage is the client—a literal household name. The kind of celebrity the word "starstruck" was invented to describe what it's like to be in their presence.

But maybe she *is* a modern-day Patty Hearst. There's no pained look of fake agreement on her face. She's asking questions. She's nodding appropriately and making the encouraging noises one makes when someone is venting their business. She is actively participating as much as she can in the one-sided conversation.

She is full-blown *present*, honey, for the full length of the trip: The sheer volume of his words is staggering. And she is hanging on to each one.

I change my mind: She's definitely a monk.

So what is the subject of his epic tale?

Money.

Obviously.

He needs it. Or owes it. Or wants it—I'm still not totally clear. But it is a tidy sum to us common folk. Tens of thousands. Cab fare from the icon's point of view, but a make-it-or-break-it number to the boy.

I say "boy" because "man" wouldn't be super accurate. He's not quite yet a man. Yes, he can legally drink—but he doesn't have the balls to handle this woman. He's so far out of his depth that he couldn't find it with a NASA telescope.

That much is clear—I can tell from the jump seat, which isn't that close to the action. It seems to be working to his advantage, though. He has the baby girl, princess-boyfriend energy that male partners need in order to maintain a relationship with a boss baddie like her. He's willing to be second string without resenting her success.

As long as mommy takes care of her baby boy.

She summons me over, again, to refill her glass of wine. Side note: I'm still trying to figure out why these glasses are so small. When I say small, I'm not even talking Montreal small. At least those are a proper four ounce pour. These wine glasses are smaller. Like, vintage cocktail glasses from the '20s meant to keep flappers from getting wasted too fast so they could… flap longer?

What are these thimbles even doing here? Can the rich and famous not enjoy a human-sized portion of an oaky Screaming Eagle?

Maybe the owners have a strong penchant for inconceivably inefficient stemware.

It's fascinating to me that she hasn't asked for a larger glass. Maybe it's so she can take a moments break from active listening.

Maybe she's sending me a message in morse code every time she taps her glass and makes eye contact.

I'd ask her if she needs a rescue—if he would ever stop talking. But that would mean God exists. It's clear that in this void, She doesn't. She's busy, I get it.

I take a moment and a few bites of the sandwich I packed for our cross-country sojourn. I must have blacked out after that; the next thing I remember is opening the plane door for a glam squad to swarm in and attend to the Goddess. Hair and makeup muscle the boy out of the way, and for the first time on the trip, he falls silent. He seems surprised that a team of people is ready to attend to her needs.

My takeaway is this: That boy had no idea how much his life was about to change. He saw his mommy-therapist-girlfriend transform into the Met Gala version of herself that you and I know from every photograph her publicist ever allowed the public to see.

Her post-plane touch-up easily costs the amount of money he's been lamenting about for the last six hours (thanks to headwinds, and Satan, I assume). His eyes betray the mental math that must have brought him to the same conclusion.

It's got to be a humbling experience.

Red carpet ready, our Goddess is ready to leave. She comes to me first.

"Thank you *so much* for taking care of us. You were fantastic," she gushes, pure light radiating from her face.

"It was my pleasure, darling," I say. She's visibly delighted.

And off she goes. She floats to the staircase, stops to give us her iconic queen wave, descends to the waiting car, and she's gone.

Despite all his noise, I'd forgotten about the boy. It was only the silence that clued me in to his departure.

I guess there is a God. She'd been on board the entire time.

CHAPTER 10

THE DIAPER

Children. Kids. Babies. Infants. Fetuses. Niños. Bambinos. Crumbsnatchers. Parasites. We know them by many names, but on a private jet they are recognized as horror royalty. They are the tiniest of terrors, the most unpredictable and most difficult to please. The children of the uber-wealthy and extremely famous are often the hardest clients on board.

Not all of them are monsters. In fact, one such non-monster was enamored with making hot towels in the galley. She was a dream. Another child had a bitch fit over dinosaur chicken nuggets. So there's a dependable, dare I say comforting, yin and yang.

There was one little Chucky doll who would not stop screaming at her friend. Said friend was wearing noise-canceling headphones and could not hear one fucking word this devil child was hurling at her—hurling at *her*, at the entire rest of the plane, and ultimately, at *me*. Her parents, to no one's surprise, were completely oblivious. Over the years, they had become masterfully deaf to their child's antics. After the ninth banshee wail of her friend's rich hippie name, I silently nestled up close to her. I waited a beat, then burst out with a loud call of *her* name (approximately six inches from her head), reminding her that the friend could not hear her due to the very large, very noticeable headphones. Not only did I frighten that child to near death, but she didn't speak for the rest of the flight. Her parents offered me a nanny job an hour later.

In their attempted poaching, they gushed about how they had never in their life, and never in the child's life, seen that little loudspeaker so quiet.

Now that we're warmed up, let's get into the Diaper Debacle.

Oh, babies. Our brains trick us into thinking they're so damn cute. I mean, they *are* undeniably cute. Adorable. Gimme that chunky lil' leg. I love all that. There's a study that came out that said our hormones trick us into believing we enjoy motherhood more than we actually do. After this experience, I absolutely believe it.

Little babies usually do really well in private jets because our cabins are pressurized much closer to what you experience on the ground. It's not so much that the infants are the issue. It's all the fucking mess of madness that comes *with* them. The number of times I have been on board trying to figure out a fucking baby carrier would melt your brain. Like please parents, help us help you. All carriers are different. We do not want to be responsible for not belting your baby in correctly. We are beyond happy to assist, but please lead the way on this. There is no class for us to learn how to strap the newest Baby Bjorn suede car seat into the aircraft. Plus, like, I don't want to break it. Or for your baby to catapult out during turbulence. Just do us all a favor and handle your baby. However you do it is fine—but *you* do it.

I say it's fine, until it's kind of like, totally disgusting and barfville gross, and not fine. I almost don't even want to tell you this next part. There's a decent chance someone is currently sipping a Diet Coke at the scene of the crime.

Crime it was. This baby was on Daddy's world business tour. Lucky bambino. The biggest perk of this family's wealth was that they could accompany each other as a family to their various engagements. Lil' bambino got to travel everywhere.

Travel is such a beautiful gift to give a child. They grow up having a profound respect for all humankind. Seeing different cultures, meeting people with different backgrounds, learning different languages, it creates this knowledge that we're all fundamentally the same. We're all one. It has such a profound positive impact on children. I couldn't recommend anything more for their development as a human.

This particular bundle of joy didn't really have much say in the matter at hand in this story. It's very much a regular baby thing to do. One of the four things they do: eat, sleep, poo, and coo. This little hot lava filled bun had no choice to let it out like babies do. His very well-manicured, well-dressed, very wealthy, very gorgeous, very ladylike and demure supermom changed this baby's diaper with such precision and efficiency, I'm not even sure she had to look. It's like it happened within the blink of an eye. She waved her perfectly manicured hands in front of the teensie babe and off came the old diaper and on went the new one.

What a fucking Goddess. Snaps for that bish.

I, as usual, have an eyeball on a client that will need assistance in the next few moments. As I floated by in perfect timing to scoop up that little pile of diaper goo with my gloved hands and throw it directly into the trash, I don't see it. I don't see those perfectly manicured talons outstretched to pass me the juicy garbage.

Where is it? *Where is it?*

Did she drop it on the ground? That would be awful.

Checks ground. Not there.

Checks her hand. Absent.

Wtf.

Checks her lap, her other hand, checks her lap again, glances beside her in the chair, peeps at her purse, examines the floor in front of her, tries to casually peer under her arms.

It's gone. That shit has morphed into thin air.

This is the Houdini of diapers. This thing is nowhere to be found. I do another pass. It's getting a little awkward. I'm hovering like a hummingbird.

Damn it.

I check on the pilots. Those dudes are fine, as always. Give them enough water, Coke, Diet Coke, or Coffee, respectively, and they're happy campers. Really what they want is a cocktail anyway.

I walk back through the cabin determined to find that damn diaper. There's no way this chick has thrown it away; that's not her deal. The nanny would have, that's for sure. I guess it's possible she passed it off to the Nanny like a misshapen football while I wasn't looking?

Nanny's with the baby now. Mom's alone. It's go time.

Breezing by *so* casually in that super calm, totally panicked way, I can see the mom's whole setup. Now that baby has switched seats, I have a clear view of the area.

As Mom is putting her seatbelt back on, I spot it.

It's reappeared.

It's somewhere it shouldn't be.

I want to barf.

This cannot be real.

The diaper is in the cup holder.

The diaper is IN THE CUP HOLDER.

Where people put their phones.

Where people put their gum.

Where people put their drinks and bottle caps.

Shiza Minnelli, I can't even process it.

Imagine stuffing a dirty diaper into the cupholder next to you and ignoring it for the next six hours.

Would *you* do it?

CHAPTER 11

FACE DOWN, ASH UP

Every industry's got trail blazers. The name sakers, the idols, the ones that everyone looks up to and are well-respected within their industry. Private aviation is no different.

Pilots are well-known for being alcoholics. Private pilots especially don't mind a roadie when parking the plane in the islands for a week. They delight in that. Drinking basically seems like a prerequisite for the job. Was that listed on a job board somewhere and I missed it? Because I do not remember learning about this in class. Coulda used a heads-up, all I'm saying.

I do remember seeing my class instructor from my seriously-how-is-this-even-legal Flight Attendant school getting drunk and recruiting down at the Marriott bar every night after class. In hindsight, I should have been able to read the writing on the bar napkin, but I try not to be one who judges. I mean…I do judge. A lot. This whole fucking book is a testament to my judgement capabilities.

But honestly, some of these guys are bordering on full-blown alcoholics. If I were at all trained in substance abuse counseling, I'd recommend they get some help. From the layperson's point of view, they absolutely need it.

Adds armchair psychologist to my business card.

In the vein of pilots being general fucking hot messes, this experience was one for the books. This book, specifically.

This pilot is well-respected. He's considered one of the most capable and experienced pilots in the industry. He's also known as a low key party boy. Everyone knows, everyone accepts it. You take the good with the bad. So what if he overindulges in his downtime; navigating a three-ton metal tube through Aspen winds and weather has got to earn some kind of grace. That shit is tough.

Guys like him have the telltale signs of a party lifestyle all over their faces. They're usually flushed with rosacea because 1) They don't use sunscreen while flying and 2) They're chronically bloated and inflamed from their alcohol consumption.

Imagine a literal red-necked pilot stuffing his leathery skinned, swollen, cranberry-looking toes into a pair of filthy Reefs, and gag with me at the visual. I have a thing about gross feet. At least now I'm not alone (you're welcome).

In case you still can't picture it: He's spent so much time in the sun he makes Donatella Versace look like a sickly Victorian shut-in. His skin is so leathery, Louis Vuitton wanted him for handbags. He shows up to the beach with more alcohol in his bag than a step mom at a soccer game. He hoards the plane's Sauvignon Blanc like a dragon guarding treasure (and he's just as generous with it).

Cut to us arriving at the airport for our first flight together. It was a big deal and to be honest, kind of an honor to fly with this esteemed pilot. After loading his two precious cases of wine on board, I discover he is a smoker. I thought I could hear it in his voice, but was genuinely surprised because pilots usually do not smoke. Maybe cigars, but I haven't met many who are chronic cigarette smokers. I didn't think much about it until I came up to offer lunch.

We are flying empty which means it's flip flops and Hawaiian shirts for the pilots. In my very casual state, with the cabin having been freshly cleaned and organized so nothing much needed to be done, I start organizing lunch. I peek up to see the Captain, our PIC, a.k.a. pilot-in-command, a.k.a. the main man in charge, crawling out of his seat. Perfect timing, I'm thinking, as he's obviously coming to ask about lunch.

I stow my knives and head his way. Halfway to him, I look up to see him tits down on the carpet.

Usually, that's not such a great sign.

I see him fiddling with a panel. Okay, he's fine, so maybe it's a circuit breaker issue?

I see the panel come off, no breakers there. Nothing to push, looks like nothing is there at all.

He's fiddling with something else. Something small.

I'm creeping closer.

What the fuck *is* that?

There's a spark—OMG there's smoke!

OMG are we going down over the ocean??

WTF is going on right now?!

Why does he look happy and relaxed?

Where is the smoke going?

My hyper-vigilance is kicking in. I have one thousand simultaneous questions.

I bolt up to him, flying through the air like a winged gazelle, if that gazelle thought her plane was on fire.

I ask him if everything is okay, and as he turns to me, I see it.

I see the fucking cigarette and he's SMOKING on the plane.

I don't know what's gnarlier, the fact that he's face down in the carpet that's rarely cleaned or that he actually knows this trick.

He explains that there's a vent right here, and it's very common for pilots to pop down there for a smoke.

It's not. It's not common at all.

It would be the only time in my career I'd ever see it.

ROSACEA

Symptoms:

facial redness and flushing, the area may feel hot and swollen, and/or have swollen bumps, enlarged nose.

Triggers:

sun or wind, spicy foods, hot drinks, alcohol, very hot and cold temperatures, emotional stress, exercise, drugs that dilate blood vessels, personal care products.

Treatments:

mineral sunscreen, gentle retinol use, prescription gel or cream or pills, lasers.

*Not always suitable for black and brown skin, red and yellow light therapy.

CHAPTER 12

BREAKFAST SANDWICH

As I walk onto the jet in the early morning, a little after sunrise, I'm feeling good. We're all prepped and ready to roll out for a book tour. We've hit a pretty good rhythm with the travel. The passengers and I have even gotten chummy, as tends to happen when you spend a lot of time together. It was my blind spot. I didn't see it coming, and I never could have imagined how the day would end.

It was still early when the group showed up. They'd been at a wrap party all night. I knew that *they* knew they were headed out, so I hadn't expected the assistant to be as hungover as he obviously was.

This assistant was prone to raging outbursts. A while back, I'd heard him disrespect his girlfriend in front of the whole entourage. It was the only time I'd seen them fly together.

He must have repeated a hundred times, to her face, that she was lucky to be on that jet and *this* is why he never invites her (it's still not clear what "this" was). He was so demeaning, so cruel, and had such revolting energy, I cannot believe she didn't parachute herself right out of the fucking plane.

That's the day I realized he was an abusive person. Ironically, he was employed by a mega celebrity who was known for their lovable, eager-beaver personality.

And yet…if we're truth-telling, the lead was kind of a loser. You know the type of guy who tries way too hard all the time, who doesn't know how to turn it off? Even when there's no one else around, he's still cracking bad jokes, filling the silence with bluster to distract you from seeing his true self.

It's no wonder he would hire an assistant like this. Opposites attract, right? And someone had to be the bulldog to his golden retriever. One couldn't turn off the schtick, the other couldn't turn off the ego.

The assistant was rejected from his former industry, where I guess he was kind of a big deal. He now made his living organizing someone else's life instead. It's cold outside of the limelight. It made him jealous and cloying. Even though he made $100,000 a year, it wasn't enough to pay for the lifestyle he currently lived, and wasn't a patch on what he made in his previous life. He was mad and bitter and hated women which, to be fair, was probably true from his first rejection or fumbling sexual experience.

So this morning, when he gets on the jet, I don't know what his problem is. He's sick of everything. I guess something could have happened at the wrap party to trigger him? I just know the man is *rabid.*

He's the last to drag his body onto the aircraft and slams himself down in the last seat of the plane. He's not a small man. It's very loud.

Startled, I look up the length of the plane and make eye contact with my favorite of their security guards. He gives me a good morning smile.

That's the last pleasant thing that happens.

"Give me a fucking breakfast sandwich," the assistant snarls at me.

Geezus fucking Christ, I think. Zero to a hundred in two seconds flat. Somehow I manage to offer a "You got it," but that's the only thing that comes out of my mouth before he's shouting again.

"—and don't make it too hot or I'm gonna punch you in the fucking face!"

I audibly gasp.

"What?!" I almost shout it. I straighten up. I'm confused, verging on scared. My heart is racing, but I turn stone still. I must have been white as a ghost.

I completely freeze.

From under the glacier, I manage to squeak out, "I know we're friendly, but you can't threaten me."

He doubles down.

"Well then don't make it too fucking hot or I'm going to punch you in the fucking face."

My anger is now verging on dick-kicking rage, but my rising fear is tempering my instinct to tackle him out of the chair and claw his fucking eyes out.

He doesn't stop.

"What are you going to do about it? Give me a fucking breakfast sandwich and don't make it too fucking hot. Now."

He does a fakeout lunge thing at me with his fist cocked. I visibly flinch.

"Or I'm going to punch you in the fucking face."

Nothing about his attitude says he's joking. His face is twisted into a deep frown. His eyes are glued to me, as if he's waiting for me to say anything else so he can unleash his wrath and pummel me into the carpet.

Wide eyed, I start looking around to the rest of the cabin. I need help.

Someone help me, I telepathically try to send to the other passengers. *Someone, do something. Say something.*

Everyone is stunned. They stare silently at me.

The lead client starts awkwardly laughing and tries to make a joke. It doesn't land.

"Danielle, just remember this: If the cops come, remember it wasn't me okay? I had nothing to do with this."

First of all, it might be local cops that carry out the arrest, but assaulting, threatening, or intimidating a crew member is a *federal* crime, baby. The FBI investigates those—and the repercussions can be fucking stiff: possible felony convictions, tens of thousands in fines, and up to twenty years in prison.

Second, there's a solid chance he'd end up on the no-fly list. It's about the worst publicity you can get when your brand is built on being Mr. Nice Guy.

I am still in stunned silence. The lead's stupid joke has ramped up my fight or flight instincts. I'm genuinely growing scared for my life. The next thing I know, I am galloping through the plane, from the galley in the back to the door of the cockpit. Tears are forming. I'm shaking.

I turn before I reach the pilots and finally speak up.

"There are nine other men on this plane, are none of you going to stay *anything* to him? You're just going to let him threaten me?" I'm fully yelling at everyone on the plane. I have broken character. I don't care.

No one even responded.

Tears are streaming, I'm shaking. Am I even blinking?

I enter the cockpit to ask the pilots for help. They're concerned, but not resonating with what happened. They flip it back to me, and I am disassociating, shutting down, imprisoned in my own mind, spiraling through thoughts of what might go wrong—what could still go wrong.

"Okay, so what do you want to do?"

They're seriously asking *me* to make the call, I think through my tears.

"Do you want to continue the trip or not? We have a few more stops today. If we report this, and you leave, that's game over for all of us."

Callous, but not wrong. If we make the call for his bear-sized threats of assault I had just endured, it might destroy everything—for both the celebrity, my career (obviously moving forward I'd be blacklisted from working with this person), and for their book tour. Plus, the blowback on the charter company and on my boss might do permanent damage to their reputation.

I don't know what to do or say. I'm terrified of losing my job. Even though they let me stay up there in the jump seat most of that day, I feel a lingering terror that he is going to punch me in the back of the head on his way past me.

Just for daring to speak up for myself.

Looking back, those pilots should have made the decision to kick him off the jet. They should have stood up for me.

I wish I would have said no to continuing. I wish I'd said that I wasn't comfortable and called in the big guns, had the scandal smeared all over the internet: This menace to society is the right hand of one of America's most beloved celebrities. They all deserved to be exposed—one for their hatred of women, the rest for their tacit acceptance of it.

He didn't get the feds that day. But you know what else he didn't get?

His fucking breakfast sandwich.

Silver linings, I guess.

When I unfroze four full calendar days later, I wrote my boss the following email. It's reproduced in its entirety, presented below with redactions, but unedited.

Actual Email from 2017

Dear [redacted] -

I'm writing you this letter four days after [redacted] assaulted me on Sunday's flight. I emailed you and made you completely aware of the situation; you called me briefly, only to say "sorry you had to deal with this. I never had an issue with him before. He's a really great guy." Well [redacted], upon much reflection of this horrific situation, I want to assure you, he is not a "great guy." I realize that when this happened you were about to take a nap, so I assume you were tired, and maybe your judgement was off, but frankly [redacted], in reflection, it's shocking to me that when I told you that a huge 6'5" former football player screamed at me that he was going to "punch me in the fucking face" and menaced me to the point that I was shaking, that your reaction to that information was to say "He's a great guy. I've never had any problems with him."

I went to the hotel that night in shock, nerves shot, still shaking, and finally broke down crying. The following days have been very much the same. When I think about the incident in its entirety now, I'm beyond upset that this man could verbally assault me like that and that nobody made any attempt to stop him, and frankly, I'm heartbroken that you never once checked in with me after knowing firsthand what I'd been through up there.

Honestly, and embarrassingly, I'm still in shock, not eating or sleeping and have been crying on and off since I got home. I keep replaying the incident in my head and remember the paralyzing fear I was in the entire day after the incident, including during both of their flights. This huge man screamed at me at the top of his lungs "Get me my food or I'm gonna punch you in the fucking face," three times in a row, along with a barrage of other expletives and mounting rage. The plane went silent. Nobody said one word to help me.

When [redacted] realized there was potential to be thrown off the flight, he finally quieted down. [redacted/the lead] tried to make light of the situation by joking "You do what you got to do, Danielle, just remember when the cops get here you tell them I'm the nice one." As we were taking off, I was still shaking, trying not to cry. I was in absolute terror thinking that if this guy gets up and makes good on his threat, I will be trapped in this plane with him forty thousand feet in the air with no one to help me.

CHAPTER 13

BITCHES' BREW

Look closely among the elite and you will see a special type of wealthy person darting between the jets they own and restaurants they feel belong to them. This person is quite the common breed (just don't tell them that). When they're not at Balthazar in Soho or Casa Tua in Aspen, you can spot them in lofts at dinner parties, sipping cocktails with whoever donated to their latest project. There's rarely a morsel in hand, but if there is, you'll never see it near their mouths. It's simply absorbed like LSD on a fingertip.

Upon closer examination, we can easily count the bumps on the bony ribcage, a pale, sharp xylophone protruding over a tailor-made pant. The pants are pinched to emphasize her teensy waist and unbelievable lack of ass. Hear that? That's her asking the cater waiter to bring her a cup of hot water and a side of lemon. The Bitches' Brew sustains her, save for the secret bites of sashimi.

These lady beasts are apex predators. They feast on the meek and thrive on the mere whiff of insecurity. These women are the tiny, hungry, *Devil Wears Prada* archetypes who might be halfway interesting if they consumed a single piece of red meat, or a sliver of baguette.

An impeccably dressed, prestigious, older client of mine is known among her crew as being…in a word, impossible. In another word: cunt. And not the fun kind we serve at Pride. On a scale from persnickety to legendary monster, she's a rung above Frankenstein's monster with twice the sutures. Nothing—and no one—has pleased this woman for decades. Maybe nothing in her entire existence. It's difficult to say since she definitely sold her soul to the devil sometime in the 12th century in exchange for disgusting wealth and eternal life.

This client, on our flight to one of her gargantuan homes, does precisely what I expect: She sits, eyes her surroundings disapprovingly, and turns her withering gaze to my happy ass, en route to displease her.

Before I can get a "hello" out, she speaks sharply and precisely, like she's addressing a child who also works for her. A child who barely grasps basic English.

"I would *like* some *hot water* with *lemon. Thank* you."

She drops her gaze back to her phone. (Her book? Her notepad full of the names of her enemies? Who remembers.) and dismisses me without another word.

Being the fabulously flawed Flight Attendant that I am, it takes a moment for me to register that our conversation is over. I'm used to a bit of banter with most of my clients, but they don't all approve of the help getting too familiar.

She can't spare another word. It's clear she is parched from verbally assaulting the peasantry. Tongue lashings really wear you out. The strain on her throat from helpfully insulting strangers must be unbearable. Perhaps she'd had an earlier encounter with a subpar Caesar salad and had to dismember a waiter. Maybe it was a noisy busboy, or a driver's heavy breathing. Can you imagine?

But she said "thank you." *Wow*, I think to myself, *she actually thanked me. Today is going to be a good day.* (Did you hear Ice Cube start playing too?)

"Absolutely," I answer and haul it to the galley.

As the kettle boils, I carefully cut and squeeze the lemon into the empty cup. I'm trying to protect her manicure from any citrusy erosion. Well...mostly.

I'm also trying to conceal another problem: The lemon is not organic. I searched multiple locations only to leave them all empty-handed. Was there a shortage? A boycott? I didn't ask. I didn't know it at the time, but it meant my fate was sealed.

The client hates pesticides. I mean, she hates many, *many* things, but this hatred is borne from a deep-seated fear of putting something unapproved into her body. Therefore, it's crucial to conceal the origin of the juice. Her ladyship would not approve. Her ladyship would have me drawn and quartered and dispersed through her kingdom as a warning to any who disobeyed her.

I pour the water. I gird my loins. I'm ready.

I approach the client, cup and saucer in hand. A spoon is balanced and poised. A napkin is present. What could go wrong?

I set the beverage down. She sighs.

Uh oh.

She huffs. She's glaring at the cup like it asked her for money.

Oh, fuck me.

"Where's the lemon," she seethes.

"Oh," I quickly answer, "I already added it to the water. Your nails looked so good, I didn't want to –"

"I want the lemon. I wanted to do it myself."

My instinct is to laugh. The list of things she "does herself" must be comically short.

Oh, shit, I think. *She's onto me.*

"Well, actually..." I begin my long, logical explanation. I am unexpectedly nervous. I'm rambling. I can feel my face warming.

I am a grown woman in fear of fruit.

The client is not pleased. She rolls her eyes, landing them back on the saucer. And hold onto your tits, folks, 'cause she ain't done yet.

"And this looks hot." It's more of an accusation than a question.

"Yes, this is your hot water with lemon," I answer.

"No, it's hot. It's too hot. I can't drink this."

I consider my next words carefully. She may not be aware that time will cool the drink.

"Oh, that's just the kettle. It will cool. Or I could bring an ice cube?"

Her head snaps up at me, face twisted. She's appalled. She's disgusted. She's planning the coverup of my impending murder. I may as well have offered to freeze my hand and finger fuck the cup to death in front of her extended social circle.

We stare at each other for an awkward moment, or for thirty years, it's unclear.

"You ruined it!"

Um, I beg your *miserable* pardon? Is she joking?

"It's ruined, you ruined it," she repeats, seemingly waving it (and me) away.

She's not joking. I'm stunned, immobilized, mute. I'm the sole wax figure to escape from Madame Tussaud.

I don't know what to do. I stammer an apology and offer to remove the offensive beverage. But as I glide my hand back toward the teacup, she grows more frustrated.

She waves in the same manner.

"It's fine," she spits. "Don't make a big deal about it, it's fine. Leave it."

I'm the one making a big deal? Is there a clearly marked entrance to the fantasy world she lives in because I'd love to get a guided tour sometime. I'm obviously kidding—she'd have me tackled by security well before I got inside.

The woman has everything except a firm grip on reality.

Fairly sure she's prepared to rip my extended arm off and batter me with it, I choose to live and retreat. I plaster on a smile and slowly back away, keeping my eyes on the wild she-beast at all times. You can never be too careful.

I don't know for certain that she banned me from all of her future flights. No one had a conversation with me about "the hot water" incident, so if she mentioned it to the higher-ups, they kept it to themselves.

I do know I never saw her again.

And as the woman is clinically devoid of joy, I know I'm happier than her about that. But I often wonder if she thinks about me every time she orders hot water with lemon. I wonder if other Flight Attendants have "ruined" her tea worse than me.

And where she buried their bodies.

CHAPTER 14

THE ABOMINATIONS

This crusty baguette of a bitch is known for being hard. Hard on you, hard on her family, hard on every person she comes in contact with. Women are finally creating their own empires—and morphing into nightmare human beings. How fun. Pretty sure that's not what our queen envisioned when she asked who runs the world.

Don't get me wrong: I am all for badass bitches.

I don't even mind an attitude. It's rough out there for women, turn the heat up to eleven and roast the room, hunty.

But honest to God, if your bitchiness comes out over a lemon…that's not "badass," that's just bad, you ass. Making lives miserable over something as mundane as fruit should be a felony. The punishment should be a *Freaky Friday*-esque, twenty-four hour life swap so the offender can get a taste of their own medicine. Those who've never worked service are the worst offenders. I truly believe court-ordered server shifts at high-volume restaurants would end the poor treatment of servers forever.

Until then, people like that walk around freely talking mad shit to anyone and everyone about every subject under the sun. It'd be kind of gangster if the act wasn't so tired, boring, and elitist. Especially over a fucking lemon.

Personally, I'm a fan. Lemons can be very handy when it comes to everything from hydration, to fish, to dressing, to aromatherapy. They're delightfully versatile.

It's the obsession wealthy women have with the lemons themselves that gives me the soul-curdling ick. For a beverage as simple as lemon and water, there's well over a hundred ways to fuck it up. I personally have experienced about ten so far, and as a good little service girl, I know it's on me to make it right. This trip introduced me to a new way.

Our poor, poor pilot. He could *not* make it right.

Some context: When you are rich but not rich enough to fly on a jet with a Flight Attendant, the right-seat pilot (the spare) must serve you drinks and snacks, even meals, while you are on board.

When I first heard this, I nearly collapsed. A pilot server? Do you know how difficult (and expensive) it is to go to school to become a pilot? Shit ain't cheap, honey. And now they're out here serving Diet Cokes and lemon waters? It's like the industry goes out of its way to humble flight crews.

Pilots can become pseudo-family members, especially if they've been with the client for a long time. They may offer to help with family, run errands, or even babysit. To ask your pilot to serve you food and drinks? That's next level. To me, that's a fucking dumpster fire of disrespect and entitlement.

In the case of the abominable lemons, this client wanted lemon with her water. Simple, right? Who could fuck that up?

Only someone overqualified for the job.

On smaller planes like the one in this story, it's standard to have the following perishable items: one lemon, one lime, a small, fresh, low-fat milk, and a fresh half and half creamer. Plus, standard onboard snacks, drinks, etc. Because of the small size, the "standard" is a very limited assortment of options. If you're not specifically asking for it ahead of time, no one is going out of their way to provide it.

There's one small lemon. Our dear pilot has one shot to get it right.

And he beefs it.

The nervous pilot emerges from the plane's tiny galley with a silver tray. He's carrying a small plate with our smaller lemon cut into six smaller pieces.

Do you see where he went wrong?

Neither did I.

Did you know there's a right way to cut up a lemon? If you said no, congratulations, you have more in common with our pilot than you thought. If yes, briefly revel in the knowledge that you know more than a pilot. On the subject of, you know, lemons.

As it turns out, eight slices is correct.

Not six.

A mistake for sure. But the way she transforms into an inconsolable, raging axe wound over his error was…a big response.

He hears the exasperated gasp. He looks up to see shock and horror contort the celebrity's face.

"What kind of person would cut a lemon into six pieces?"

"Why would I even *want* these? It's an abomination."

Our confused pilot begins to apologize, to tell her that it's these slices or nothing, but she cuts him off.

"Throw them away."

She continues to light him up from his toenails to the tip of his perfectly coiffed hair. She needs him to not just understand that he was wrong, but that what he's done is a crime against humanity. A war crime. An unforgivable slight against the human race. (For those of us who didn't know about the eight-slice rule, maybe we can all carpool to The Hague later? I'll post a signup sheet, let me know.)

When our pilot returns from throwing out his shame, she's ready for the second tray of lemons. She's shocked.

"I still want lemon with my water, go cut another," she hisses.

"As I was trying to tell you, that was the only lemon we have," he answers.

The expressions that cycle silently across her face are priceless. She, defeated by her own idiocy, realizes she's pulled an Icarus, reddens a bit, and slumps back in her seat.

Sometimes karma is a lemon.

TRAVEL TIP

Bread goes stale incredibly fast in flight; be sure to keep it sealed until ready to chow down. If a baguette goes stale, simply run water over it and pop it in the oven for a few minutes, it will be good as new.

CHAPTER 15

ENTOURAGE

Let's set the record straight real quick, right here and now, for clients, for God, for country: I JUST WORK HERE.

On the flight back from an event, you would have thought we were riding in a hatchback. This overgrown six-man entourage could not contain their disgust with the size of the jet. They were appalled that I would put them on a plane of this size. Me, the lowly, powerless Flight Attendant.

It's laughable they could even imagine I would have that kind of power. I didn't choose this "little ass plane" for you and your crew.

Your boss and your boss's spouse chose this "little ass plane."

I had nothing—literally nothing—to do with it. I was simply assigned to be Igor the butler on this ego-filled trip. I guess part of that includes having a new asshole ripped over something I can't control.

The person I'm standing in front is...upset. "Livid" and "enraged" almost describe their state. Apoplectic is a little closer. I'm listening to them berate the absolute shit out of me. That's not normally part of my job, but this is an important client. So right on cue, I'm disassociating my way through it.

Even though I'm still not responsible for it.

"Why is that plane so small? Why would you force us into this tiny fucking plane? We're going to have to share the space!"

Sweet Jesus in a Prius, you guys will have to sit next to each other?! Will you even survive?

They go on for several minutes, despite my assurances that I am just as perturbed by the size of our plane, and that I did not choose it.

It has no measurable effect on their conviction that I am to blame, and I must be punished. Do they ask about the dumbass, LA-Instagram-inspired dietary restricted meals that took a full six hours to source?

I'll give you three guesses, but you'll only need one.

Most shocking of all? This person was not the client.

This person was part of the entourage.

See, these entourages have usually been together for a while. Some of them have been there from early success or possibly even childhood. The ones that go way, way back are the ones that *really* push the envelope.

When placing orders for food, it goes like this: The person who is paying for the jet—or said person's wife/mistress—sets the tone. They choose what's eaten, when it's rolled out, and generally how much each person is going to get.

So if you're hungry AF and the point person has decided not to put the buffet out until mid-flight, then you'd better get your ass up and make best friends with the snack basket. By the same token, if you're all expecting to eat, but you're not eating buffet style, then the lead client, wife/mistress, and children will always go first.

Respect, hello? It's called decorum, people.

If you need to eat before the lead, I'd once again refer you to said snack basket. Raid that motherfucker for all I care. Stock pile those snacks in your cheeks and save them for later, IDGAF. But you'd better not be asking to eat ahead of your boss.

And, duh, there are some caveats. If your boss has given your ungrateful ass the okay, or you're being very rude and putting the Flight Attendant in a very uncomfortable position, that rule is going to bend a little.

But it goes like this: The leads will place their order and everyone will follow behind, much like a restaurant. Unlike a restaurant, the food will come out in chronological order, the way it was ordered, rather than all at once. Mostly because I am not a kitchen, these are hands, not wands, and there's only one of me. I'm working with what I've got, and in the tiny galley of a private jet, it ain't much, honey.

Now that we've gotten that out of the way, let's get back to this flight. One member of this entourage believes himself to be as important as the client. Or at least on par with the spouse.

Spoiler: He's wrong on both counts.

Still, the who-even-are-you-level passenger has the boss's blessing to speak to people (me and the other members of the entourage) as though addressing a steaming pile of beach garbage. I suppose they'd known each other long enough that it had become the *de facto* tone. It somehow translated to treating me the same way. This was equal parts endearing and infuriating. It was nice to be accepted—but it was superficial acceptance, because at the end of the day, I worked for them. And boy were they keen to remind me of it.

And not to be a raging cunt about it, but AS IF I would voluntarily work with them! I'd rather live off of lizard bones and malaria water than take a job inside the warped, mean-girl cult of drama these grown men created.

One of them was a truly cancerous mole. His stank attitude was souring the group and had been causing an unstable dynamic for years. Having also flown them for years, I had seen the devolution. It was fascinating…it was also disgusting, considering the brunt of his resentment fell to me, the inside-outsider.

Again, we'd been doing the chronological food parade for years. But on this trip, the man-princess decides it's unacceptable.

And so it begins…

"Man, it'd be nice if I ever got my food. I'm so hungry, you'd think I'd be able to get my food," he's complaining to the entourage.

"Your food is coming, I promise," I say, smile frozen to my face, holding eye contact a few moments longer than Emily Post might approve of.

"'Promise?'" he says mockingly.

I resist a retaliatory eye roll. *Baby's cranky when he's hungry.*

The other members of the entourage are exchanging looks. They can feel something brewing, but here's a fun fact you don't find out until you've worked in the industry for a while: No one on any flight will ever take up for the Flight Attendant. No member of the entourage will intervene and no client will discipline one of them for barking at the help. It's just not done.

"Jesus, it's been, like, over an hour," he's barking as I literally approach with his plate in my hand.

He's lucky I didn't mash it into his fuuuuhking face.

"Finally," he groans, rolling his eyes. "I'm starving over here."

"You are?" I feign surprise. "You should have said something!"

His eyes bulge out of his head. I thought he was going to leap out of his seat and slap me to death with a ham sandwich.

Another guy in the group snickers.

Thank God he survived.

So strong.

CHAPTER 16

LEFT BEHIND

*I arrive at the airport to find twelve cases of Perrier-Jouët bubbly waiting for me. It's a standard order for this trip to the Four Seasons in the Jungle. It's stunningly gorgeous there, but you simply *must* bring your champagne with you, darling. Of course.*

I survey the inventory. We're bringing those twelve cases, plus an extra half case to nurse hangovers on the return flight. We're also bringing enough food to stock a small Erewhon. Between the food and the imminent passengers, the jet is about to be packed like a Japanese train car during rush hour, or the L train to Manhattan at any hour.

There won't be one open seat on this motherfucker, which suits me just fine. It's going to be a busy trip, and I love it. I thrive in that kind of environment.

Let's go, bitches!

This stylish group is particularly fun because it's a whole bunch of super kind, polite, low-maintenance twenty-somethings who want to party for the six-hour flight. That in and of itself doesn't make much sense: A group of almost twenty people where *everyone* is cool? It's hard to believe because it almost never happens. The lead passenger himself makes even less sense.

He enters the plane first with the rest of the passengers following like a conga line. He makes his way to the very back corner seat by the galley (that's my domain, remember) and immediately whips out a giant book. That thing was THICC, like an Instagram model's BBL.

The man is instantly immersed in it. He's not waiting for anything or anyone, not even a glass of champagne. He's clearly anxious, possibly a nervous flier. People do what they have to when flying is a chore and not a pleasure. For some, it's two bottles of wine. For others, it's two pounds of weed. For our lead, it's the biggest book ever printed. Good for him.

A bubbly, pig-tailed girl with a spray tan joins him at the table. She's saying a thousand words. I'm hearing more tone than substance, but from the uptick at the end of most of her sentences, it's clear she's determined to engage with him.

She looks adorable in bubble-gum-pink, but turns out… it's not going to make every man wanna take a bite. Especially this lead.

He could not have been more uncomfortable. He's attempting to be polite, but he clearly does not want to engage. I chalk it up to a fear of social situations. It's not uncommon with highly successful people.

I'm walking through the cabin handing out glasses of champagne after takeoff. Usually, I would offer beverages beforehand, but never ever on my precious sanity would I do that with seventeen passengers all under the age of thirty and new to private aviation. Judging by the copious amounts of selfies, it would seem it was many of their first times. I love to pop that cherry with them. I get off on making their experience as enjoyable as possible. Thank you therapy for guiding me through the realization that I am a people pleaser and that's why I am so damn good at this.

Finally handing out champagne, I get to the front of the plane, the last six glasses teetering on a silver platter with my free hand holding the bases down for dear life. Everyone who got there late sat at the front of the plane.

Side note: Never show up *late* to someone else's jet. Just don't do it. Show up a day early if you have to. A month. Set up camp in the FBO. Change your mailing address and your driver's license and host a house warming, but never show up *late.*

As I'm teetering with the tray of champagne, Mr. Number Seventeenth Passenger inquires about the nature of the bubbly. Requesting the name specifically before deciding if he will join the sixteen other passengers and his generous host for a toast. I was simultaneously joyfully amused at his unabashed arrogance and absolutely annoyed at his downright rudeness.

Jokingly, as I serve him a glass anyway, I muse that next time he wants to be picky he should bring his own champagne. A satisfying round of laughter erupts from his friends, his scowling little frown said he had accepted the burn but was not defeated. His Cartier love bracelet with diamonds says he is in love with no one but himself. His dismissive nature exposes himself as an asshole.

At one time, I would have reveled in taking this dude down, but honestly, who the fuck even cares. I have sixteen other passengers awaiting a refill and some hors d'oeuvres. You know though, you can never outrun sweet, sweet karma. It's a dish served unexpectedly, and in this case, swiftly. A true joy to witness.

During the in-flight party that ensues, there are many a glass of champagne poured, many a shot taken, and thankfully, many a story told. This is how I found out that one of the girlies on board is a roommate of the owner and her boyfriend is on board, too. The roommate loves to share his wealthy lifestyle and encourages her to bring a boatload of her hot, young co-ed friends to his gorgeous home in an island paradise.

Now, looking back, I'm almost certain she was a lucky sugar baby and he let her have a boyfriend as well. I think he was some kind of nerdy voyeur. Maybe a little unsure of himself, or maybe packing a teeny little weenie itty bitty short broken-off chode of a penis. Looking back, I wonder about a million things.

Especially when they continued, trip after trip, to invite me to their house to party. The adventurer in me of course wanted to go and soak it all up. The Goddess in me knew that they wanted me to partake in their little trysts. Zero part of me wanted to be eating kitty or sucking dick and then have to look into their eyes while serving drinks and food to them on the way back.

But honestly, everyone that knows I'm a Flight Attendant immediately thinks that is my life. Little do they know, it looks more like long days serving joyless clients followed by a glass of wine and an early bedtime.

The reality is rarely as glamorous as people imagine.

As the seventeenth passenger would soon find out.

He was too arrogant for this group and his mere presence kind of surprised me. He was rude in all the wrong ways and charming in exactly none. I gave him the bare minimum attention while making sure the rest of the passengers had a rip-roaring good time.

We finally land.

Everyone grabs their passports and excitedly shuffles out of the plane and down the stairs. The pilot is leading the charge and I am walking back with the lead passenger over to customs. We'll get them cleared and head off to the hotel. I'll be poolside with a cocktail in about three hours, I think.

Everyone is cleared and I see the lead passenger looking around. He looks…annoyed. I see that, in fact, not everyone had cleared customs. It's Mr. Seventeenth Seat.

Customs is shaking their head. They're aggressively saying no to something. As I'm walking over to speak with the customs officer, Mr. Seventeenth Seat is throwing his hands in the air in disgust. It's getting heated.

I step in and find out from Customs that little Mr. Seventeenth Seat was too busy flashing his self-love bracelet to have double checked how his visa works. Apparently, he was on a new visa that was less than three months old. According to this local customs officer, he can absolutely travel out of the USA on that visa, but to travel into Costa Rica, the visa must be at least three months old.

While the lead passenger ushers the last remaining of his remaining friends into the van to head to the Four Seasons, we leave Mr. Seventeenth Seat sitting at the airport.

I later found out that he would be held overnight at the airport as the last flight back to the States had just left and the next one was twenty-four hours later.

That's what being a cocky, Easter-Island-head-sized dick gets ya.

CHAPTER 17

MORNINGS

It's time to get up.

But what time *is* it, specifically?

You know, "starting the day" is a relative term. Sure, the majority of people work a traditional 9a.m.–5p.m. And granted, the sun rising has generally signaled the start of a new day for…well, I guess, since forever? But hush with the logic—those are just facts. Pretty convenient facts, if you ask me. Too convenient. It reeks of an agenda.

It's pushed for and championed by people who live in a set routine. They need the world to be in tacit agreement with their belief in the One True Start Time. Non-traditional workers, those who work graveyard shifts, hell, even evening shifts: We're all threats. We undermine to the stability of the Cult of Mornings.

These are the thoughts in my head as I attempt to puzzle out the time.

What even are mornings anymore?

I'm swaddled in a sea of crisp, luscious hotel sheets. You know the kind. Thick and white. They engulf you in a kind of sterile coziness that's better for sleep than a tranq dart.

Is it still morning? I think it's 11 a.m. or 12 p.m. ish—hard on the ish. That's local time. I try to do the math on what time it is in the States. Carry the one, minus five hours (or plus three hours?) cross a handful of time zones…fuck it, I'm too tired.

A few minutes ago, I sat up in a dead panic, convinced I was missing a flight. This is pretty routine. Lately, I've been averaging twenty–twenty-five flying days per month, every month. That is a mind-shattering pace. I was meant to only fly about fifteen or twenty days, max.

My days "off" had turned into prep days between flights. My downtime was virtually nonexistent. I'd been running hard for months. My adrenals were all fucked up, so when I slept, I went down for the count. Narcolepsy. Corpse pose. If I'd been alive a few centuries ago, they might have mistook me for dead and buried me in one of those graves with the little bell on top.

Time was losing meaning. Recently, the dead-sleep-to-full-tilt-panic-mode was happening more and more. Mornings seemed to last at least half of the afternoon. I might wake up just in time for happy hour at the hotel bar before venturing out for dinner-breakfast.

I'm lying in this bed, mulling over the last couple of days. I count up my hours: nineteen hours over a thirty-hour period of time? That can't be right. I count again. The math is sound. It's what happens when taking two very high-profile VIPs on two very important trips.

Okay, *all* trips are important trips (massive eye roll), but these two are special for reasons I'm not at liberty to disclose.

Yesterday, after landing at the second location—a tiny island where you definitely wish you were reading this book right now—we were escorted to a fantastic resort. Looking back as I write this story, I appreciate it. At the time, I was too sleep-deprived, too mushy-minded to give a tropical fuck. When we got to the resort, I dropped into the bed…but I didn't fall asleep.

What the hell is wrong with me?

I was overtired and over-hungry. I *couldn't* sleep. I couldn't remember the last meal I'd eaten. I vaguely recalled wanting In-n-Out back in LA, but not having time to get it.

Snap shot memories. I saw myself laying on the floor of the cabin in the middle of the night, also not sleeping. I wanted to be fresh so we could land in this undisclosed island revitalized in the morning.

Hahaha, "fresh." I roll my eyes. I haven't been "fresh" since I started flying 25 days every month. This look is held together with hemorrhoid cream and a Sudafed washed down with an Excedrin Migraine.

The clients need us looking happy and well-rested. And you want to show them that side of you. For the crew, you can roll up looking like an eye-lined zombie in a lipstick. No one gives a shit.

I must have gotten at least a few minutes of sleep, I justify. *Let's go get this sun—that'll wear me out for sure.*

I wrangle myself out of the bed, slather my hot bod in sunscreen (sunscreen is SO IMPORTANT, people!), and head down to the pool.

There are a number of loungers open. I zero in on one in full sun. Target acquired. A couple of people are waving at me, and it takes a moment to register their faces. It's the pilots in

Tiki-patterned shirts. They're flushed and grinning, several frozen cocktails deep at this point.

I point at the lounger. They nod. I flop down and close my eyes. A few minutes later, the pilots walk over with a drink for me, too.

"Hey, Danielle! I can't believe you're awake right now!"

Neither could I.

"We're about to order some lunch. Are you hungry?"

So hungry I could eat the glass my drink came in.

I join them at the table. The shade feels wonderful, and the drink is hitting the spot.

Ping.

I look down at my phone.

Oh right, I remember. *My boyfriend.*

For the last forty-eight hours, I hadn't thought about him, not once. I didn't have room for him. I had been wall-to-wall with the client's needs, travel schedules, and catering.

But a bunch of missed calls and unanswered texts later, my time is clearly up.

Ping.

The pilots notice me, my expression, as I'm looking at my phone. They ask about it, point blank. Pilots are nosy AF. They love them some gossip, and they were drunk enough at this point to own that. I start to explain that this boy I was seeing kept calling me over and over and texting and badgering me to call him—when he calls again.

I answer.

"Hi, I'm sorry I—"

"I can't believe you've been ignoring me," he starts in on me. "That's so unfair."

"I told you these couple of days were going to be really hard, and that *I* would call *you* when I had a chance to take a breath. Do you remember that?"

"Yeah but it's been two days. I mean, you haven't had *any* time in *two* days?"

I literally haven't.

He's not having any of it.

"I just can't believe that. With *my* job—"

"You're a personal trainer. You take clients for an hour or two at most when *you* feel like working. It's not the same."

"I can't believe you would say that. You think your job is *so much more* important than mine."

"I literally don't. You know I don't."

"Then why can't you call me?"

The reception outside is terrible. I'm starting to catch every third word. I try to convey that I don't have the braincells to have this stupid conversation. I was about to hoover a couple of freshly cilantro'd and limed tacos and pass out by the pool. He can't or won't hear me.

He wants to argue. I hang up.

I set my phone to airplane mode and stop responding. I need another cocktail and a dip in that turquoise pool STAT. I don't care that we are at the public pool at an all-inclusive resort (our clients were next door at the *truly* luxury one) where people are definitely pissing well liquor at the swim up bar. Regardless, I need to be in the water.

Somehow the time doesn't pass. It's noon for at least three hours. A few drinks in, tacos settled, my phone blissfully silent, I can feel myself getting drowsy. I consider staying where I am, on the lounger in the sun.

But that bed…I need to be in that bed. I wave goodbye to the pilots and high tail it to my room. I feel like I have some energy, but I can also feel sleep tapping me on the shoulder. It's bizarre. I can't explain it at the time. I would come to find out that is called "adrenal burnout."

Sweet darlings, don't let a job push you to this stage. It's truly not worth it. It happens with too much stress, like routinely staying up all night, working night flights, and traveling in and out of time zones.

I am feeling out of sorts: Wired but tired.

This is the perfect time to call my man back, I think. *Maybe he'll have calmed down.* I optimistically scroll to his number. He answers on the first blip of a ring. I immediately know I made the absolute worst decision. He is pissed.

Now, he's not the first guy I've dated while flying, and he definitely won't be the last. On this call, he's giving me the usual crap guys give me when they feel I've shirked them once I've gotten to my destination.

"Did you have fun by the poOoooOoOol?"

"Did you MeEt aNy GuYssss???"

"ANYONE BUY YOU A DRINK?"

"OHHH tHe PiLoTs ArE yOuNgGgGG aNd SiNgLeEee!?!??"

Oh for fucking fuck's sake. I immediately stop him. Nope. No, shut it down. We're not doing this. It's not happening. I'm dead tired. I'm on a work trip. It's not a vacation. It's never a vacation. I've been up for thirty-six hours and I'm so tired I literally cannot sleep. I need him to get on my team, trust me, believe me, and use some logical judgement. So he does.

He powders a wig, grabs a robe, and judgmentally asks:

"When are you going to start making *me* your priority?"

I resist the urge to immediately hang up.

This is a *fucking* man-child. I explained my job to him when we first met. He pressured me into being exclusive. And this is not the first time he's berated me for not having time for him.

Which, I explain, is why I didn't want to be exclusive.

Awkward, yes.

Less awkward because we're on the phone, but still.

He throws such a pissy bitchfit and is so selfish and immature that I'm at the end of my rope.

I drop the news:

"Look, I know my job sucks. It's been hard on all my relationships. I'd been planning to surprise you: I have a few days off after this trip, and I was going to spend them with you. But you're such a selfish baby about this. You're the opposite of support. I can't do this anymore."

I promptly end the relationship.

He tries to take it all back, as they do (amiright, ladies?), but it was too fucking late. He pushed too hard. He broke it.

I hang up the phone and lay down on the bed.

I finally, almost immediately, fall asleep.

CHAPTER 18

TAKING THE PISS

This chapter...it's so gross that I put off writing it until very late in the game. Buckle up folks, it's gonna be rough.

Let's talk hygiene.

I know everyone has a different definition of it. Some guys don't wash their hands after they pee. Some people don't clean the bottom of their plates or their legs (you should). I saw a girl on a podcast talk about her "weekly shower," wherein she only washed her hair and let the runoff take care of the rest.

Yes, she was white, because of course she was.

For some things, hygiene is a moving target. Other things are cut and fucking dry.

So let's get into it.

By this time in my aviation career, *cringe* I feel like a boss ass bitch at work. I fully have my shit together. I am well known for my positive attitude and respected for my work ethic. I do no harm but I take no shit.

Well...I *think* this is what people think of me. And I hope so, especially since I just declared it to the world.

As you know by this point, working a charter trip lands somewhere between absolutely delightful and an inescapable nightmare. Despite appearances to the contrary—this book is mostly documenting the worst experiences—most charters fall into the first category. The people were usually at least a *little* bit of fun. They're hitting major cities and exotic destinations with their nearest and dearest. Plus, flying around in a private jet is like the western world's definition of "making it." You're gonna have some fun with that—how can you not?!

Believe me, some don't.

This client...they own their own jet. Better yet, they own a fleet of planes, along with a helicopter (or two?). This is a big deal. Helicopter money is in a class of its own. Jet around the world all you want, but if you can't afford to cosplay a villain hanging from the rope ladder of your own helicopter, you're gonna be called poor by someone.

And it's not just multiple aircrafts. The client is particular AF. If you're working in any official capacity with them, it's more than likely that one of their multiple assistants sent you their four-page rider in two languages, just in case you'd like to read it in Mandarin.

Let the record show I do not speak Mandarin.

They cc Flight Attendants on an absolute novel of an email/welcome note that looks helpful but feels threatening. The instructions have been cobbled together over years of mistakes. In order to avoid future fallout, the client's team details his expectations at great length.

But these long messages are the ones I appreciate the most. People who own their own planes can be extremely...I want to say "detail-oriented," but I'm landing on "high-maintenance." They're just *particular* about their lives, their service, and their surroundings. I like particular people. They will tell you exactly how they want it. There's no guesswork, no request to improv. It's beautiful. Most of the time.

The coffee, for example: He wanted Espresso a certain way.

"It's Nespresso," his assistant wrote one afternoon in an email. "Double checking to make sure you have the machine on board."

She reminded me, again, that he wanted two black Nespresso capsules.

"Capsules—NOT PODS."

I'm to press the button for a larger size. I'm to use one pod each time. Under no circumstances am I to run one pod twice. He *will* know. It *will* be a disaster.

Send a spoon with his SINGLE USE NESPRESSO CAPSULES.

They said the brand name like they were paid per reference. But reiteration is key to memorizing something. They wanted this implanted into my brain like the Kars4Kids song.

Got it, darling: NESPRESSO.

Ping

Another email.

"Double checking the Nespresso Capsules."

You get it. We'll fast the fuck forward.

The client walks onto the plane like he owns the bitch, which he 100 percent does not. For all his aircraft, this jet is a rental. Make it make sense.

Tall and broad, he certainly looks intimidating. For the next hour or so, I'm trying to figure out what's so bad about him. He's well-dressed, polite, and confident. He seems fine. For all the breathwork I did to prepare myself to survive a

Freddy-meets-Jason style nightmare scenario, he's pretty low maintenance.

Possibly a Type A assistant? Or maybe he holsters his bad attitude around new people? It would make sense…

Anyway, there doesn't seem to be much wrong with him…a lot of build up for an anti-climactic finish.

When we land, he isn't giving me any indication of how I performed. He doesn't tip (shock), but he also doesn't provide much feedback.

But what he did in the bathroom makes me think he fucking hated me.

The man—the grown, responsible, extremely wealthy and capable man—sprayed his piss all over the lav like a cat marking its territory. Everywhere.

It was like his dick had twelve holes, or maybe it resembled a colander. Maybe he had three dicks at different heights, like those showers with multiple heads.

I swear to Christ on a bicycle, I've never seen anything like it. The color, the smell—Lordt, the smell—the way it looked like a bloody crime scene except instead of blood it was neon piss. The man was *not* well, honey. I was *shook*.

It's not like we'd had turbulence! There is no logical explanation for how or why he decided to paint the room like he'd brought a supersoaker full of piss. To this day, I am mystified by it.

For all the detailed correspondence with his assistants, you'd think his kink for putting out imaginary bathroom fires with his hole-y dick would warrant a mention.

If this was his way of showing me he was unhappy: Message received, loud and clear.

But damn, next time just use your words, bro.

CHAPTER 19

THE HITCHHIKERS

Flying into Van Nuys is such a treat for me. I love the West Coast, party-in-the-sun-but-not-in-Florida vibe. Granted, the airport is nowhere near the beach. But all of Lost Angeles has the vibe, even places deep inside the Valley.

I'm on the jet by a window facing the tarmac. After prepping the other seating areas, I'm doing the final touches for the client—fluffing, monogrammed pillows and matching blankets on the seats where the lead likes to sit. Out of the corner of my eye, I see something. Something moving fast.

I look up: A line guy is hustling out to the plane. He's, like, booking it. That's never a good sign. I check the time. It's way too early for passengers to show up, plus these fliers are usually right on time if not slightly late, so it's unlikely to be client-related.

The line guy sprints up the stairs, abruptly stopping before his oily black boots hit the cream carpet. I've moved to the door to meet him.

"We've got passengers, if you'd like to come out and get them. Not the primary. Are you ready?"

Super-bleh. I hate this question. Am *I* ready? Yes. Is the cabin ready? Also yes. Do I want to spend an extra millisecond servicing the demands of passengers playing king for a day? Absolutely not.

As we have already learned, parts of an entourage require higher levels of maintenance than the lead. I honestly think it's because they're finally getting the treatment they feel their proximity to greatness entitles them to. I get it. Now that I've retired my lil' wings, there's a chance I'm about to become the neediest of passengers. Siiiiiiike. Once you work for monsters, if you have any kind of self-awareness at all, you become keenly aware of how *not* to treat others.

I disembark and walk back to the FBO. Inside, I spot the two little dingleberries who showed up early. They are beyond delighted to find out we're still in the first phase (well, pre-phase) of boarding.

They are delighted to be the first to arrive and aggressively desire to be served.

I have an inkling that the passengers hitching a ride are first-timers. No one in the main entourage ever shows up a full hour early for the flight: They're part of a well-oiled machine that all tend to get to the airport within minutes of one another, like clockwork. The entourage doesn't hang around the FBO, or sit on the plane for an extended period of time, because time is money. It's the one thing they can't buy more of.

The girlies' fits are adorable, if somewhat impractical. Don't get me wrong, I love a good stiletto, but if you're not used to strutting around on the polished floors of an airport you wind up moving like a tiny T-Rex. Not to mention that the heel will get chewed up when you're hoofing it across the tarmac, which means you'll now stand a better chance of snagging the overpriced onboard carpet. High-heeled footwear is a classic rookie mistake. It will totally give you away.

If you want to travel like a pro, wear a sneaker.

I'm trying to figure out who these little gangly, upright antelope are as they teeter-totter their way toward me. I check the manifest again. They are not on it. But they *are* looking like two newborn baby gazelles navigating their long knobby legs for the first time. It's genuinely funny, so I decide to humor them.

When I tell you these bottle-of-Saint-Tropez-self-tanning-lotion skeletons *demanded* entrance to the 90 degree jet, I'm not doing the performance justice.

I approach them with a "Hey, ladies—"

One cuts me off. "We want to get on the jet."

"Of course, but it's hot in there right now, FYI. You're about an hour early if you're flying with—"

"We were invited," the other one chimes in.

"Yes, when you were allowed through the gate I assumed you'd be on one of the jets. We can go out, but because you're a bit earl—"

"We're flying with [REDACTED], and they said we could ride with them, and we want to go on it before they get here."

I stare at them both for a moment then flash a smile.

"Yes, I understand. Alright, let's do it, ladies!"

And off we go, passing out of the FBO doors toward the waiting aircraft.

Now, I don't typically like to see people struggle. I'm a helper. I'm likely to jump in and offer some kind of assistance before you've even asked.

However.

It's pretty satisfying watching these two try to navigate the tarmac on their own. Besides, how could I have helped? Carry them?

Not on your fucking life, bro.

Their clawed hands are white knuckling their iPhones as they struggle from the FBO to the staircase of the plane. It's about three hundred yards. Not far in sneakers, but it would feel like three miles in the wrong shoes.

I'm easily outpacing them in flats, so when I get to the stairs, I stop and turn toward them, ready to wait.

Their expressions are a mix of determination and frustration as they hobble toward me— I can tell they're trying to make it look sexy and effortless, which…I mean who's that for? It's only me here, and I'm not gonna fuck you, girlie.

As I wait, I try to imagine their game plan. If they thought crossing the tarmac was tough, they're in for a treat when they realize the pilots don't turn on the jet until we're preparing to leave; and we're certainly not burning jet fuel to save two Insta-Angelistas from sweating out their hair extensions.

Once onboard, they are sweet. Saccharine sweet, like, overly, painstakingly polite. It's like their brains are trying to force their features into kindness, but the eyes and mouth can't quite nail the expression. They don't smile: they show teeth and squint hard.

It's difficult to look at.

They "ask" for Chardonnay (without using a question mark) and complain about the heat.

They flop onto the seats with the monogrammed pillows, because of course they do. The white, pristine, steamed pillow suddenly hits the floor and homegirl is literally stomping her knockoff Nudistsong heels into it.

People are so fucking ratchet.

Before I can even pour a glass of their Midwestern housewife Chardonnay-with-ice cubes, I had to attempt to rescue these pillows they were kicking to the floor and trampling with their Zara stilettos. It sounds stupid to try to explain why these pillows matter, but they do. And I can't let a couple of Duane Reade divas kick the custom embroidery to the floor because in about two hours, the lead will be rubbing their face all over it.

They are mid-photoshoot when I return with drinks. They do not pause to receive the wine. I'm just standing there like an idiot while they pout and preen (and sweat) and snap a hundred selfies. Only when they stop to review the session am I able to serve them. Again, they show teeth and squint their thanks.

I step away, snatching the pillows from under their heels and a minute later return to check on them—the wine is gone and they're ready for another glass.

Perfect! "I'll be right back."

That's when I see it: globs of drugstore lip glue, I mean gloss, stuck around—*all* around—the rim of both glasses. It's so thick that I can't wipe it off. I need straight acetone. I need the dish soap used to wash oil out of baby duck feathers. I've never seen anything like it.

Fuck it, I think. *I'll just pour new glasses*. It's a quick trip and the boys should be here soon. There's no way I'll run out.

An hour and several rounds of Chardonnay later, I've run out of glasses.

It's fine because the boys are finally here and I'm getting prepped for takeoff.

We load everyone in and that's when I see it.

As she bends over to hug the lead, her leggings go entirely see-through, exposing her dried little raisin to the all of us.

I go temporarily blind from the surprise clit attack, and think to myself, I don't get paid enough for this.

CHAPTER 20

SUPER BOWL

I don't remember falling out of the car onto the pavement, but I do remember waking up covered in vomit to no phone, a body full of bruises, and a very sore throat. I was also hella thirsty and hungry and thank GAHD it was only Saturday and I could get Chick-fil-A. I don't remember if the pilots brought me some or I ventured out on my own. Maybe it was delivered? I'm not entirely certain.

Really most of what I remember started when I saw them in the lobby of the hotel at some point during that next day. I feel like it was later in the afternoon, but I was still very out of it and my mind was moving slowly. It was creeping through quicksand to some blurry memory of sitting at the bar waiting on the pilots to arrive. We had all said we'd be heading downstairs, confirmed as we were walking out of our rooms.

Cut to met sitting at the bar solo, like so many other nights out on the road, two texts buzzing in declaring both dudes will be right down. They're close friends, so their schedules are the same even when they're not. And unless they're running a ten-minute train on some rando, they're having a quick convo with their wives and kiddiwinks. I'm ignored at the bar for a minute and I think nothing of it. Happens all the time. A bit strange when it happens during Super Bowl weekend because usually the waitstaff are primed, pumped, and ready to make that tip, baby.

Not this chick. She kind of avoids me, it would seem, even when I'm smiling directly at her and making eye contact. Whatever, I'm distracted by the pilots texting anyway.

The bartender rolls up to the bar and all of a sudden she's the friendliest person I've ever met. She's beyond friendly. She's thirsty for my order and my attention. Weird. Lady bartenders almost never make that turn so quickly. Maybe she had a change of heart, I think.

I order a skinny margarita and notice a beady-eyed man in a bright neon yellow-green jacket sitting to my left, STARING at me like I'm a prized pony. I am, so it wasn't unusual. But, it WAS annoying. Super annoying.

I remember feeling like *back off buddy, it's never going to happen.* Never, not a chance, not if you grew two feet and spawned a Hemsworth face. Not if you had a gym body and a God's dickle. Never.

There is a waitress serving the tables behind me in this Atlanta lobby. I remember her presence, but that's it. I couldn't pick her out of a lineup of waitstaff.

The pilots show up by the time I am about halfway through my cocktail. We were going to have a drink or two and ride out to dinner. I vaguely remember another girl came with us. She was a Flight Attendant too who sometimes flew with my pilots but happened to be in town with another crew. I remember her being very pretty, but a total bitch… she wore the bitchiness like armor. She was just young and likely a little insecure.

We order another round. Midway through my second drink, things start to brown out. I must have decided to get up to go to the bathroom. Judging by my camera roll, I thought the lighting absolutely *fucked*, because my cocktail and I were having the Vogue-iest, high-glamour-in-a-gross-location editorial shoot in history.

My eyeballs did not show up to the set ready to work.

In most of the photos they look like they're trying to see behind me through the back of my skull. In others, they're running away from each other like teams playing capture the flag. In others still, they're leering down at the lens like some googly-eyed Amazonian deity.

I find my light (even when I've been roofied, turns out) and if my eyeballs could have found the camera the pictures would have been sick, bro. Instead, I looked like someone slapped googly eyes on After Party Barbie.

She's sold with her gay best friend, Rough Trade Ken.

G sold separately.

Allegedly, the story goes like this: What's her name, the one with the mean, pretty face, came in to get me because we were leaving the hotel. Apparently, they had been waiting a while for me. The pilots sent her to find me and bring me to the Uber.

She finds me dancing and talking about how much I love this song, which, in all fairness sounds exactly like me. Even sober, I love me a dance party. I think she eventually drags me to the car. I insist on taking my watered-down cocktail with me, and off we go. I remember sitting in the middle. And our Uber was a woman? That stood out…I think.

What happened to the cocktail, you ask? Well thank God I brought it. Otherwise, I wouldn't have been able to spill it all over everything and everyone in the car within one minute of climbing inside.

Because of course I did.

Thankfully the pilots had plenty of small bills to tip her.

Now we're en route to dinner. Allegedly.

Smash cut to me wobbling in front of the restaurant. After a thirty-minute car ride you would think I would have sobered up a bit, right? Me too!

Turns out, no. Hard no. Like the hardest no. It would just continue to get worse. Because I wasn't drunk. Not off of two drinks. Not with my lifestyle, honey.

It also gets more disgusting.

Just as one of the pilots comes over to ask if I am okay, I turn my head and start projectile vomiting.

The entire front of the restaurant is glass. Forty to fifty people set their forks down to watch me recreate a scene from *The Exorcist.*

I guess I was trying to be polite and covered my mouth with my hand like hiding a whisper. In fact, a raging river of fluids violently shot out behind it.

At this point, the crew was over me and my seemingly drunk ass. This was extremely evident when they told me they called an Uber and even though I was apparently still puking my face off when the driver came, these three ignorant assholes dumped me in the car with a stranger and LEFT ME. What a bunch of tools. The girl was obviously very selfish, just from like, her entire personality. Such a bitch. The dudes though. They had children, they have girls. They let a stranger take my clearly blacked-out brain back to the hotel.

That's where their part of the story ends. Well, except for the fact that they attempted to text and call my phone to no avail as I, like a drunk girl in a cab, left it behind. Eventually, they called the room phone, I answered, called the pilot, the other pilot's name multiple times aaaaaand fade to black.

When I wake up fully clothed on my bed…well…I wish I could tell you because I was STILL blacked-out. Really, the only thing I know is what the pilots told me. So fucking scary. After scarfing down Chick-fil-A, which I feel like was courtesy of the pilots guilt, still unsure, I roll up to the place that had my cell phone.

It's a little mall inside a Walmart-type building. It reminds me of a huge flea market I once went to in Austin. There are all kinds of clothing stalls, a thrift shop, and little Bodegas. My guy is a Moroccan dude and runs a bodega in the back. When I get there, he explains he is relieved to know I was okay as I had been in such poor shape. When I opened the door to exit the car, he said he watched me crumble to the pavement and had to get out and help me up. I then stumbled into the lobby and he watched me get into the elevator, before unknowingly driving off with my phone. He was surprised the people I was with let me leave alone in that condition.

Uhhh, me fucking too! People can be the worst. This crew flies for a young billionaire. One would think one would be more responsible. When we talked about it the next day, the consensus was that basically they thought I was drunk and I'm an adult, had done it to myself, so I basically deserved to be left like that.

What would *you* have done?

CHAPTER 21

GIRL ON A PLANE

I used to fly this one client. Straight businessman central. He ran like clockwork. Never flew too early in the morning or too late at night. He always showed up on time. Easy meals, very low maintenance. The dream client. I LOVED flying this dude.

One fateful day, I'm looking over the flight manifest for this beloved client when I see a name. It's an extra name. It's the name of his girlfriend. And it's a name I fucking recognize.

It can't possibly be the same person.

Can't it, though?

In a previous life, I'd worked at a medical spa. The name I recognize was a frequent client of my spa. She was kind of infamous with the staff. Not only was she wildly entitled, rude, and transparent in her singular goal of locking down a rich sports player, she treated other women like...like something standing in her way. An inconvenience. A threat, maybe. Competition. And I, for reasons I can only guess at, was her favorite place to lodge that hostility.

That was back then, years ago. People change, I think.

Do they, though?

I won't lie. The day of the flight comes, and I'm nervous. I don't really know what to expect. If she's dating my client, she failed in her desire to climb a ladder of jockstraps to sportsball heaven. Well, failed upward, like so many terrible white people before her.

They show up to the plane. I'm warm and welcoming. The client greets me like an old friend.

"You always make my flights so easy. It's great to see you."

I'm happy to see him, too. Happy to see that, despite the girl he's joined his life to, she hasn't changed him. We still have great rapport.

Then I see...her. Well, to be fair, she's seen me. She's gone white (whiter), as if the fat from all her old liposuctions has come back to haunt her.

She's thrown off by my easy relationship with her man. She eyes me up and down. She opens her mouth to bark an order.

"Hello. Wine. White."

Surprise, surprise. She's the same nightmarish, social climbing gremlin she was all those years ago. She is exactly how I remember her, which, to be fair, is not extremely detailed. I remember her pre-injectable mug shot. I remember her inability to remember my name, despite seeing me regularly.

I still can't really believe she's flying on the same freaking jet I work on. The universe has a sick sense of humor. Like, what the actual FOOK did I do in a previous life? It must have been bad. I must have been a warlord and orphaned a village. I must have murdered the last unicorn. Or invented central banking.

How had I come *so far* only to end up serving the same clout-obsessed Regina George's of the world? It isn't fair.

If she hated me more than 100 percent of the time back then, she hates me 200 percent of the time now. If hiding your distain for others was an Olympic sport, she would never place. If unabashedly chasing rich men was an Olympic sport—let's be real, she was always gonna get the gold. The gold of some poor sucker. Even if she had to *Gone Girl* a few people to do it.

Ugh, the poor suckers.

If she even *attempted* to call you by name, it sounded like she was trying to use it against you. You may know someone like that. Someone who thinks they're doing a good job of pretending they're not insecure—who, despite a Bentley's worth of plastic surgery is still ugly on the inside.

Every gesture, every expression, it all reeks of desperate behavior. When I knew her years prior I was *so* embarrassed for her. She had a lot of growing to do. Despite being ten pounds of asshole in a five pound bag, she always seemed to land on her Louboutin clad, perfectly pedicured feet. That fucking bitch.

On the plane, I got one lil' taste of her shittiness and all the memories came flooding back. I remembered it vividly. What a drain on the soul this chick was, how I dreaded her showing up at the spa. How she made simply asking for water sound condescending. Her vibe was just so palpably bad.

The first evening after flying her, I ran to my hotel room and collapsed on the bed in tears. I truly could not believe that I was having to serve this monster of a human *again*. She watched me like a botoxed hawk when I served her man. I could feel her staring at me if I ever moved into their line of sight. She's on high alert constantly.

To be clear, I did not and do not have any interest in her man, AT ALL...but I don't understand how she, this absolute yawn of a hag, could bag a man that seemed so relatively cool and normal.

This chick who managed to be rude without even speaking. This chick who flat out just refused to use my name back in the day and would continue the trend any time I flew her. It made no sense. The universe must have spawned her into my new life for a reason. But that reason eluded me.

I tried to be compassionate. Women like her have little power in their own lives. They use petty tyrannies against the world because it gives them a taste of the power they lack. Deep down, they are supremely insecure.

It's why they barnacle themselves to influential people. Without that, who are they? A closet full of designer fits without the personality to pull them off. It must be painful to understand just how truly replaceable you are. The clothes, the jets, the mean girl persona...it's a wall around the deep, empty hole inside her.

That realization gave me some solace. I dried my tears and had a fitful night of sleep. In the morning, I would have to endure her again.

And the hits would just keep coming.

On this flight, she's brought a gaggle of girlfriends with her. They're drinking, they're laughing, they're living that housewife life, despite not a solitary wedding ring amongst them.

And they're getting familiar with me. I'm being adopted into their ranks, against my will and better judgement.

Some of them even follow me into the galley to hang with me while I prepare the meal. We're girlfriends now. They're opening up to me like Disneyland at dawn.

The shocker of the century comes when Evil Barbie joins us. She's acting strangely. She's standing so close to me I can feel her breath. And the way she's staring at me is new. It's not the same glare. It's softer, somehow.

She goes perfectly still. And then speaks.

"You know, when we lived in [Censored], I was in love. Did you know that?"

Me?

Why would I know that, honey? *How* would I know that? I had once met the man she was talking about. He was a wealthy sugar daddy, wrinkled like a Shar Pei, but not nearly as adorable.

She says it again, her face soft, her voice pitiful: "I was *so* in love, and I really thought I was going to get married. We were *so* happy."

I look at her girlfriends. They're staring at her, all concern and understanding, slightly nodding. Then she suddenly looks at me, dead in the eyes (and dead behind the eyes).

She stops speaking. Well, stops spinning a hindsight narrative. But, she is still looking at me. She's giving me a wanna-be People's Princess stare, but it's giving more Bitchy Barbie than meaningful gaze.

She's waiting for me to say something. And she'll be waiting for a long time. It's all very out of character.

There's so much awkward eye contact coming from this girl that I'm actually confused. Then I'm worried.

Oh God, is she having a stroke?

I start going over the F.A.S.T. acronym for a stroke: Is her face drooping? Kind of, I mean she looks weird AF, but has she always looked like that? I can't remember.

Does she have arm weakness? Ummm idk, I mean, they're folded in front of her as she's boxing me in here.

Is her speech slurred? A little, but that's the alcohol. This bish has zero speech deficiencies.

Then it dawns on me. This is a show. She's acting—*for me.* I'm almost touched, but it's genuinely funny. She knows that I know who she was, how she was known for using men to get what she wants. How the old boy she dated was a placeholder while she searched for an athlete who could provide a similar lifestyle.

Holy fucking hell: She's kind of afraid of me.

I have information that could fuck up her relationship with the client. Hilarious. I let her continue, trying to focus on her with large understanding Bambi eyes.

"It was a really different time for me back then and it was a really hard thing when it didn't work out."

Oh I bet it was.

It's hard when that credit card that pays itself off disappears. Please girlie, fucking spare me.

I met him, I saw you together. You weren't in love with him. You were a destitute pick-me who loved his lifestyle. You're that same pick-me now.

She's never met a woman that didn't threaten her, the same way she's never met a rich man she couldn't swindle.

Compassion hits me again. I let her spin me her new reality. If a girl wants to marry a rich dude, I want that for her, too. I'm a feminist, and a femiYESGETTHATBAG, honey!

But for her…I was offended that she thought bad acting and a poorly concocted backstory would wipe away the years of suffering I endured at her hand.

If I could say one thing to all the girlies like her, I would say this:

You can fool some of the men some of the time, but the way you treat other women says everything about you. It will follow you. It will show up when you least expect it. We're cognizant enough to see through your sheer shirts. We know that you picked a newer, hotter, younger, richer target and hung around until they stopped asking you to leave. Just like you did with the Shar Pei. Just be fucking for real with the girls. We'll remember your true nature like it's your mug shot.

But, I guess she had forgotten.

Or maybe she was a better actor than I give her credit for.

How to Spot a Stroke

BE FAST

Balance Loss: sudden loss of balance, dizziness, or walking differently

Eyesight Changes: vision loss in one or both eyes, blurry or double vision

Facial Drooping: uneven smile, drooping face, or numbness

Arm Weakness: weakness in one arm or leg that can't be held up straight

Speech Difficulty: slurred speech, trouble speaking, confusion, or talking nonsense

Time to Call 911 / 999 immediately

CHAPTER 22

A PILOT'S TIE

If pilots had a creed, it would be... bring us your snacks, your cold drinks, and warm meals, your finest cutlery, all desserts on earth, and endless, handcrafted barista-level coffees during espresso hour (didn't even know there was such a thing). There'd also be a line about using the bathroom in the back of the plane while the clients sleep. For no apparent reason.

There's a common joke in the industry that goes like this:

What's eighteen inches long, black, and hangs in front of an asshole?

Answer: a pilot's tie.

Funny? Kind of.

Accurate? You bet your sweet tits it is.

Pilots can be the best and worst parts of the job. In that way, they make or break the spirit of the crews. They are often more entitled than the clients, which is a feat in and of itself. They're generally overworked and have therefore earned the reputation of being (and, honestly, the right to be) cranky. Broadly speaking, they're usually impatient, white fifty-somethings who believe the world was literally made for them.

Mostly because it was.

A lot of private jet pilots came from commercial airlines, or in some cases, the military. I don't want to say their job is cushy—Lord only knows the stress of navigating a plane through torrential weather—but compared to being a fighter pilot or doing search and rescue, piloting private jets is the cushy-er option. They sit for hours on end, snack themselves stupid, and while they do not have an easy job, I would argue it's a hell of a lot easier than dealing with a plane full of people. I mean, *I* don't have an autopilot feature.

Now, before you start tweeting about how misogynistic I am, I have legit flown with only two female pilots. That's over the better part of a decade.

Not a joke.

So yes, when I talk about pilots, I'm specifically talking about the male variety. All of them in this book are men.

What I would have given for an all-female crew…

As we have seen with the #MeToo movement and #TimesUp, we know that working with men can be a …challenge, shall we say? Or a dick-riddled hellscape?

Aviation is very much a patriarchal environment. Is it a daily pissing contest? Easily. Do pilots require nursemaiding? Guaranteed. Most days, it feels like I am babysitting giant newborns. I make sure they're drinking enough. I check that their bottle—I mean coffee—is the right temperature, with the right amount of cream-to-sugar ratio. Have they gone to the bathroom before we take off? Do it now—it'll be a whole thing later. I'm forced to un-consensually mother them. it's not my favorite part of the job.

Pilots of a certain age are pretty devoid of social graces. Slight inconveniences by a normal standard can fully ruin their days.

I flew with a private pilot whose infamous line was…wait for it…"I hate change." Meanwhile, Change is the singular guarantee of private charter.

There are one hundred changes before a charter flight even takes off. Why would you get into corporate flying to be at some wealthy person's beck and call if you hate change? Like, I am genuinely asking at this point.

Hate it or love it, as Flight Attendants, our appearance factors into whether we get hired or not. It's a massive factor. Yes, it's superficial, but presentation goes a long way in the industry. It will determine who we fly, on which planes, and how often. Get a reputation for looking sloppy and it will follow you.

I'm not just talking about being classically attractive; there's a lot of heavy lifting that goes on behind the scenes. We're the face of the operation. The clients want to see polished perfection. A fellow Flight Attendant of mine would have clients commend her on how expertly her nails were done every time she flew.

In contrast, pilots put virtually no effort into their appearance. They don't have to. They might comment on how much effort *you're* putting into your looks. They might mock you for being *so* focused on your hair, nails, and outfit. They'll dismiss justifications with waving, unwashed hands and dirty fingernails.

So often, the pilots, with their grubby stubby hands, would ask you to do things for them. Dumb things, like throw their trash away. Every single male South African pilot I flew with would reach out to shake my hand. Well, the appearance of wanting to shake my hand. And in the process, he'd put a tiny piece of trash in my palm.

For me to throw away.

I don't know how they can move under the crushing weight of their infinite audacity.

My *favorite* example became a routine experience.

A pilot asked me to find his oranges and bring them back to him. After rooting around in his bags, I returned with a handful of napkins and his requested fruit.

He stared at the orange, then looked up at me.

"Unpeeled, darling?"

My eyes narrowed slightly.

"Are you *not* going to peel them for me?" he whined.

With this manicure? I am certainly fucking *not*.

What's most ironic about the men who are in charge of jetting people around the world is often their total lack of interest in other cultures. We often stay at incredible resorts in developing countries. They can't always cater to the creature comforts pilots expect as if they were stateside. Pilots seem to almost always forget the fact that we are at the mercy of what the island provides.

On a five-day trip to one of these said islands, I was with a snarky and stubborn pilot. The snark came from his all-meat diet. Veggies are Beta.

He opened that carnivorous trap once and lectured me that *vegetables were bad for you*. My face must have betrayed my brain. I may have also accidentally called him ignorant, judging by his gray-ass face.

He proceeded to chomp at me like a rare steak.

"It doesn't matter what color the vegetables are either, they're *bad* for you…"

Mmmmkay..

His meat of choice? Chicken wings.

Naked, bald-ass wings of chicken. No sauce. No flavor. As boring as he was. And of course, instead of organizing his own specific delicacy of nude chicken wings, he instructed me to do it.

If I sound bitter at all in this, it is only because I am. Super bitter and twisted that caretaking and serving others is one of the most disrespected positions in Western culture. Shown to us so easily in how we take mothers for granted. How we've been taking our essential workers for granted.

This barnacle of a man was so intense about his nude chicken wings that he gave me my very first (and second) panic attack.

He also had very intense feelings about his coffee. One morning, having breakfast at the resort, he made the server make his coffee FIVE SEPARATE TIMES because according to him, she couldn't get it right. I guess doing it himself never occurred to him? Or more realistically, he's the world's biggest, pants-shittingest baby.

Grow up, dude.

I'd also like to point out that he didn't tip a single person on that island, even when we made the airport open early to leave. He said, "Why should I have to tip people for doing their job?"

What a gross fucker. I still have nightmares about that grey, muppet-looking motherfucker.

That muppet wasn't the only one with a specific diet. Pilots have all kinds of strict eating habits. Some are vegetarian, but only eat processed "vegan" foods. They won't touch actual fruits and vegetables.

Cali pilots are counting their macros and micros, bruh.

We've got lactose intolerant pilots that eat cheese and could use their death farts to power us halfway around the world. They'd like half and half in their coffee, please and thank you.

The more run-of-the-mill restrictions are gluten-free, sugar-free, or pork-free. Many are under the assumption that processed meats are fine, but sugar is the issue; so much of an issue, in fact, that they believe fruit is bad for you.

They're usually the same pilots that drink alcohol and order extra chocolate, whipped creamed, artery-clogging desserts every evening.

Three tiramisus...one fork.

And no tip.

CHAPTER 23

SEVENTH TIME'S THE CHARM

This guy. You can tell he's used to being pampered. You can tell he's used to having his way. You can tell that at this stage in his eighty-plus year old life, he doesn't even have to ask for things to be done his way. His staff just knows. They have to. Otherwise, they'd be fired.

His wife is the same. For all her wealth, when it comes to shelling out for anything, she's as watertight as a frog's ass. If she can start a fight over nothing, and get out of paying for anything, she's having a good day.

Once upon a broke bitch time, she fancied herself a spiritualist who really understood the meaning of it all. Now, she's just another entitled white lady who lives to make everyone miserable. She must have taught him the tactic he pulled with me.

This flight was standard for the Mr. He flew to LA regularly. Like most old money New Yorkers, he dabbles in business on the West Coast.

Side note: Once upon a time, this dude was a hottie *for sure*. You can tell it in the way he speaks. He's got that confident glint that betrays he has no clue he's aged out of flirting. It's cute, mostly because it's not predatory.

It would be cuter if he tipped. I can't pay rent with your sparkle, gampy.

Turns out, like an early 2000s pop star, Mr. is known for liking a good ole Starbucks Frappuccino (hold the whip). He decided he would like one on today's flight.

Just FYI, that should be on his rider!

But, no problem, I aim to please. I confessed that I did not know how to make such a concoction. I mean, it's coffee obviously, duh, and like...milk and sugar...right?

How hard could it be, I thought, walking back to the galley with a perma-smile on my face.

Turns out, it's hard. Props to baristas around the world.

I tried googling, but of course, every last drop of the WiFi onboard was being slurped up by the plethora of devices it takes for these guys to work. I'm winging it.

I get to work cooling some coffee, getting some sugar and ice in the Magic Bullet I carry with me for exactly such an occasion. And I blend. And it looks weak. Like tea with more than a splash of cream. It looks like a milkshake. I taste. It's like if a Jägerbomb were made with milk. I cannot serve it.

I dump it out and try again. This is looking better.

By now, it's been more than a few minutes. Mr. is getting impatient. He wants to taste it. Now.

I'm hesitant, but I can't exactly tell him to hold onto his old balls for ten seconds while I dial in the recipe.

I present the beverage. It's a solid miss.

But, he appreciates my effort. He wants me to try for a third time. And no throwing it out before he's tasted it. He wants to taste every single mistake along the way.

"This is not how I do things. I am supposed to have this down to perfection right out of the gate!"

He laughs but I can tell he's bored and enjoying this game. Plus, I catch him staring at my ass when I walk away. It's not great, but at least he's not shrieking at me.

Fourth Frap. Still a hard pass.

Fifth Frap, getting closer, he says. Consistency is there, flavor needs help. As I walk back to the galley for the sixth time, his youngest assistant gets up.

He said he's found how to make it. Thank the coffee Gods because honestly, I'm not sure how many more times I can make one before serving lunch.

I read the directions and realize, I was never going to get there. A Starbucks Frappuccino requires powdered instant coffee. This was before TikTok made it the must-have that it is today—or was for its ten minutes of fame.

But you *know* I'm prepared. Your girl is a wizard genius. I grab European instant coffee from my bag.

Mr. has never been so delighted. He raves. He praises. He finally shuts the fuck up and drinks his coffee.

CHAPTER 24

THE STRADDLE

I have never seen such a large man on such a small sofa with so many people. I know by now you're thinking, ooooh who is this large man? You're never going to guess, there are so SO many huge dudes that no one's heard of. This is one of those dudes; he also happens to be extremely wealthy and very generous.

This guy brings a boatload of people with him every time he flies. It's always very casual and everyone is easygoing, having some low-key fun. He's nearly always the last one to show, like any good host, and all his guests are always situated and waiting for his arrival.

This trip, I notice that a very small man, I'm talking 5'6" if he was standing on his tiptoes in ballet flats, has spread his tiny body over several seats. I don't recognize this young man from flying with us before.

Later, I find out he's someone's assistant.

BECAUSE OF COURSE HE IS.

Why *wouldn't* the smallest, least significant person on board take up the most room? Duh! We are on a private jet of course, it's *Alice in Wonderland* rules up here. Nonsense makes sense.

Honestly, from looking at their interaction, I think they were DL lovers. Such a shame because they would have made a super cute couple...you know, minus the fact that he was so supremely selfish.

In the packed plane, he makes the largest dude sit in a seat where the Flight Attendant had to straddle him to get past...

Ummm, wait a second.

Uh-huh. Ohhhhhkay.

So, I'm just really getting this now as I write this story.

That was the whole point.

For me.

To straddle him.

The whole fucking flight back and forth through the cabin.

I'm an idiot.

Next.

CHAPTER 25

BOTTLE SERVICE

Guys are like…kind of the worst. That's not news. I mean, do you think every friendly smile means she wants to fuck you? Definitely. Are you generally always sweaty? Yes. But, are you sweaty like meat sweaty from breakfast sausages, also yes. Especially old college buddies who get together once in a blue moon to play golf when the head brosef himself invites them on the jet he rented.

There's always one. One that married early, has always been faithful, always been a tad overweight so the ladies never flocked to him so he'll always have the sting of being green when it comes to the ladies. And the Flight Attendants, it would seem.

This particular walrus of a man came from a good ole flyover state somewhere in the ass-end of who-gives-a-fuck. If Vegas had odds on it, I'd bet the farm that his beard smelled like old ham salad and 7–11 cigars. The man's in serious need of an electric toothbrush. And a haircut. And a beard shape. And a manicure and pedicure and who the fuck lets this man leave the house looking like a late-stage Howard Hughes?

It's clearly his first time on a jet. And here he sits for his big debut on his college buddies' trip with the hot Flight Attendant. It's the cliché he dreams about when he's stuck back by the toilets on Delta.

He's ready to party.

The poor, bloated dear. I almost can't even blame him except I fucking can because please have manners as grown-ass men. PLEASE. As women, you have forced us to finally beg you—and here we are begging you—to grow TF up and stop treating us like objects you want to fuck. There's a 99 percent chance we do not want to fuck you. If we wanted to, we would. Period. Now you know why no one's fucking you.

Ahem! So this poor bastard dear is overcome with sheer excitement and reverts back to his college days when he was shotgun-beer drunk, bragging to his buddies about how much ass he wants to tap. Sadly, we all know, he never ends up tapping it WHICH IS WHY HE IS NOW harassing me on this gorgeous, multi-million-dollar tube hurtling through the air with zero escape hatch.

By now, we all know that a significant part of my job is hosting onboard: offering beverages, the notorious Diet Coke, specialty cocktails, gourmet meals, and gorgeous buffets. The requests are endless. This group was having a buffet-style party at 43,000 feet in the air. Consequently, there was an enormous amount of my 5'9" modelesque self, bending over in his and his buddies' general direction.

By now, this cumbersome sea mammal had already had a beer or two (at most) and clearly could not control himself. As I bend over for the last time, he reaches across the conference table, beer bottle first, aiming directly at my derrière.

Over my shoulder, I hear him say how much I want him to put that bottle up my—

WHAT NOW?!

I'M SCREAMING INSIDE MY HEAD.

Instead of immediately turning around and using my fists to show him exactly how unwelcome he and his beer bottle are near my temple of a being, I pause. I am a lady at work, after all.

After a large inhale and a slow exhale, I abruptly turn to meet his gaze. I calmly explain that he is dead wrong to think my delightful derrière blocked the booming sound of his lewd declaration. Unfortunately, at this time, I would have to decline his most gracious invitation to enjoy that bottle and suggest that he think twice before speaking again.

The man has never been redder in his lonely, misogynistic, sex-deprived life.

There's a chance his friends are still laughing at him.

CHAPTER 26

BORROWED MONEY

It's funny the things you hear when the elite speak freely. The conversations they have. The hills they die on. The jokes they make. The fun they poke at each other.

You've probably known a mean clique or two. You may have even been their target (God knows I have been).

Honey, let me tell you, those experiences were like sitting in a cave watching shadows on the wall compared to the 3D torture I witnessed on a routine basis. Like if pettiness grew up.

And of course, it would be level one hundred in the private jet community. Everything here is about blowing the back out. It's always who has the bigger jet, or who got the bigger deal, the best price, the biggest bang for their billion bucks. Who's making the most money, who's evad—ahem—*saving* on taxes the most, who has more in the bank, who spends more on strippers, on women, on drugs, on gambling, on poker, on traveling, on fucking. Who has the biggest, the smallest, who lost the most, won the most, has the youngest girls, the hottest girls, the raunchiest pictures from their side pieces.

The real race is who can grow the biggest ego, but unfortunately, no quorum can ever form a consensus. Plus, they're all kinda winners there, in my book.

Most of the time, it's just one giant pissing contest among the trust fund babies of the richest people on earth. Their parents or their G-Maws and PapPaps started fine (old), decent (racist), companies ranging from the furniture you sit on to the banks you stash your cash in, from your favorite sports teams to those overpriced jerseys and jeans you wear. And a whole golden spectrum of niches you've never once even thought about.

You would never be able to name them and you'd never notice them if they walked by. That's by design, too—*their own* design. You aren't meant to. It's not *for* you. Everything in their demeanor says the world is tilted in their favor; if you don't threaten that, or can't enhance it in some way, I believe they are literally unaware of your existence.

Prove me wrong.

But to call it a parallel universe is inaccurate. We aren't living separately; it's more that they live in the impenetrable void at the center of our shared reality, almost exactly how scientists describe Sagittarius A, the Milky Way's black hole. And how getting mixed up in either will warp you fucking senseless.

During one of these lil' trust funded joy rides, we're flying to Vegas for what's about to be a night of pure debauchery. Based on the barely legal, superheated Snapchats flashing around the cabin, the guys will have company. I glimpse photo promises of what would be waiting when we landed. Are the girls of age? Their tattoos say probably. I'm giving fifty–fifty odds that they're legal to drink. The trust fund "boys" are mid-thirties to -forties and nerding out because they're Snapchatting with young hot chicks while their wives are MIA…sorry, *in* MIA.

But step back in time, before the flight. I'm in the galley, I have clear instructions. I'm making...wait for it...peanut butter and jelly sandwiches. Because the man-babies are gonna need snacks for later and they're not that into broccoli. Or fidelity, turns out.

I am following the rider to a T. And yes, I was instructed to cut the crust off of the peanut butter and jelly sandwiches. For adult men.

It crossed my mind to leave one triangle crusted, you know, just to see what a snack time tantrum looks like as performed by one whole grown-ass man. But I only glanced down that road: Something well-funded and unmedicated stared back. Yikes.

In their crustless form, I saran-wrapped the living fuck out of the Kidz Korner sandwiches so they wouldn't go stale (frequent fliers know what I'm talking about). I suddenly felt the pitter patter of size eleven feet on the stairs.

Expecting a dumpy, grown up, boy scout troupe, I was pleasantly surprised by the relative normality of the guests. A few were even downright attractive, objectively. I might even have sent one or two a Snap back myself, under different circumstances. Tens of thousands of people fly private every year and often bring their hot friends. That is what we like to see.

To be honest, you never really know what to expect before the people show up. Names don't tell you a damn thing, although we are provided with the weights of all the passengers on board.

That's right: remember when you gained three pounds and the stress of thinking someone noticed made you physically gag?

I noticed, ya bish.

So as our group boards, I'm clocking wedding rings, I'm catching second phones, I'm seeing Snapchat tiddies while bags *are still in hand.* They are going to Vegas and they are Going. To. Get. It.

They are fully fratting it up in the cabin. Lots of chest pounding and the aforementioned endless pissing contests. The lead had money, sure, but it seemed like any one of the crew could have bankrolled the trip.

Meanwhile, in at least some of these early photos, the boys are making obscene hand gestures with visible wedding rings. It's a genuine possibility that the Snapchat thots didn't know they were the steamy side piece. There's a greater possibility they just didn't give two fucks.

It's just another little idiosyncrasy. To listen to these masters of the universe talk about it, you'd think they just discovered sex. I guess it's locker room talk? As a woman with no locker jock-ular experience, I can only hope this doesn't betray some well-guarded secret of Men. But real talk, is it always like the comment section on PornHub? Just awkward and giddy and full of truly shocking adjectives? Don't answer that.

ANYWAY (stop distracting me) the real gag comes a few months later.

Another specific rider, another trip for a different trust fund/finance/independently wealthy gang of giant children, although they were unmistakably younger. And when I say vicious—look at me—you have no idea. Marvel villains could take lessons.

So they're on the plane, they're loud as fuck, they're talking all the shit about all the people who aren't physically present. A name comes up.

It's the name of the client I'd flown a few months back. Spider sense activated. Listening level ten.

And oh the shade was DARK, honey. Apparently the crustless bunch were often the subject of ridicule within the broader private jet community. And like the ghost of Christmas past, accompany me to a window, where inside…

"Oh, you know who's a real piece of shit?"

"Who?"

"[Censored] and his fucking pig family."

"Dude tell me about it."

"Right? You know his family made all that [Censored] money, like, thirty years ago. That was them."

"I know. And they still buy everything on fucking credit."

"Because they have no fucking money."

"That's what I'm saying. They don't have cash. They have credit."

"They have credit. Exactly."

"Poor assholes."

"Seriously poor, I mean dude, it's all on credit. I mean maybe they have like twenty million dollars in the bank."

"Maybe."

"Yeah. Maybe. Fucking assholes."

"Fucking assholes."

"We should buy them out, take all their shit."

"You would fucking own that family."

"You get it."

I get it.

You can be a *part* of the elite without actually being considered elite *by* the elite. You and I live on the outside—in our eyes, that echelon is solid. But it's not. There's more space between the gradations of the wealthy than there are light-years between solar systems, and having millions in the bank still makes you trash in the eyes of billionaires. To them, it's almost worse than having a five-figure salary: At least those people aren't *trying* so hard. It's hard to figure out which is the greater sin: being at the bottom of the 1 percent or being labeled a poser try-hard.

If you didn't suckle luxury from the tit as a baby, you may as well be an alligator wrestler from the Everglades.

The worst part was the laughter. It's always the laughing *at* that comes off the harshest. Something about the eyes, or the inadvertent snarl their mouths make when they're ripping into another person. Cackling and howling...remember when the *Wolf of Wall Street* crazy-laughs at the idea of getting his boat seized? Multiply that by ten American Psychos and we're hitting the level of mania that would describe this laughter.

Is this comedy? It's hard to say. My instinct says no, but I'm not part of the black hole that this humor appeals to. I'm not laughing. I'm off in the background being horrified. This kind of multi-generation elitism is *bred in*, honey, and there's not a mental health expert in world with the tools to unwind that problem.

Unfortunately the problem, unlike the humor, isn't confined to one devastatingly influential section of society. The balm of "everyone struggles" just doesn't hit the same when you start to consider the casual conversations that take place in private. I'm not sure anyone should have the power to destroy a whole family out of spite, and while my opinion is relatively worthless, the ideology isn't.

At the end of the day, it's hard to see what kind of joy comes from the jockeying and slamming. You'd think it'd be tainted, like a glass of happiness contaminated with arsenic. It's tempting, and it's right in front of you.

But is it worth it?

That humor, as shocking and cruel as it often is, is pretty emblematic of the greater problem here, and you don't need perfect eyesight to see it. Is there a certain amount of dehumanization in every job? Sure, but we're not talking about forgetting there's a barista behind every Starbucks order. This is wholesale reduction on a level usually reserved for intergalactic villains and superhero nemeses.

And it's not rare. I regularly listen to full monologues from pilots making a quarter of a million dollars talk about the *real* problem with poor people, or black people, or women, or how immigrants *are* destroying the fabric of this country, actually, and how *if* I disagree with the way Americans run their country, I can fuck myself right off.

And what's the takeaway from all of it?

Ego.

Me.

Me first.

Me only (if possible).

Me at the expense of you.

From the mouths of rich white dudes around the globe, we hear them chant this single, self-sustaining syllable. "How will it affect *me*? *I'm* not paying for that. Sure, they're suffering, but I can't worry about that. They should have tried harder. They should have saved better."

Tell me, is it reasonable for the average person to "save up" for a private jet? The highest levels of wealth will simply be unattainable to the vast majority of us. Maybe it's for the best. Those ecosystems spawned active sociopaths armed with violent sums of cash and shitty dispositions.

At a certain personal valuation, your morality blinks out of existence. The heady aroma of arrogance and ability can resemble invincibility. These are the men who see themselves as Gods, and you and I as instruments. Or toys. Or…fleshlights.

Definitely fleshlights.

CHAPTER 27

JOURNAL ENTRY #1

Presented raw and unedited for your amusement.

The audacity. Where TF these people, these elite entitled motherfuckers, get off is BEYOND me. I cannot even comprehend this level of assholeishness and selfish fuckery the elite possess.

We are mid-pandemic. And by mid, I mean we're eight Goddammed months into little to no work, living on unemployment, and barely making ends meet when this pilot has the AUDACITY to tell me that according to the new management company, the Flight Attendant is "required" to pay for all of the clients catering OUT OF THEIR OWN POCKETS. On their own credit card or debit card. Because this is mid-pandemic and your dear essential workers are hanging on by their fucking teeth. God forbid you throw them a bone and let the pilot's company credit card pay for these assholes' caviar and Veuve. Fuck me and then fuck me again if I say yes to these ridiculous terms of employment. I'm actively trying to get off of government assistance and you're like fuck it, have them buy my Caymus wine and salmon. Fuck you and fuck you AGAIN. Raw. Zero lube because are you out of your Goddamn mind asking the only person NOT on payroll to front your wealthy client's food for their private flight because GOD FORBID they actually have to sit next to someone. I cannot use enough cuss words right now. I hate this job so much. But more than the job, the people are the fucking worst. The dregs of fucking society. The teet suckers of the wealthy. It's fucking gross.

The stupid-ass pilots that secretly resent the wealthy people they work for. Wait a second…that might be me. Sike. That is 100 percent me. Right now, I am so fucking resentful that these companies would even ASK let alone REQUIRE someone not on payroll, someone who they are using on a contract basis, to subsidize what are routinely two hundred thousand dollar trips.

For most of my career, I had an awesome boss. Favorite Boss hands down. He is the BOSS of all bosses. He's a handshake kind of a dude and I love that about him. That's also what made me take the job because, to make deals based on relationships like he does, you have to follow through. He had his accountant pay me immediately, always. No exception. The expenses were never disputed. I did once let my credit card run up to $19,900 before submitting three months of expenses. Like an asshole. Who does that!? (Wow, okay, stop judging a bitch and listen. What I know now is that because traveling nonstop led to a drop in all my hormones, the result was crippling and overwhelming anxiety when it came to that intimidated me. Numbers, math, and money. Okay. So. Thank you for understanding.) Obviously I was reprimanded because oh my God that is totally lazy and unnecessary. Expenses scare the shit out of me, I hate doing them, and I always find random-ass receipts later that I had misplaced in a hurry that ultimately has to come out of my pocket. That's totes my bad. I worked an insane amount of days a month and had zero personal life, so at thirty-five I made the change to go contract, a.k.a. freelance. That means I can fly for anyone at anytime, not just my boss and his albeit impressive roster of powerful and celebrity clients.

I was looking for what we in the industry call a Part 91 account. That means you work for one owner and are in charge of stocking the plane, usually the stock room too, and helping maintain the entire inside of the cabin. Think everything from phone chargers, headphones, and sodas to blankets, seats, and carpets. Don't forget my favorite part of the plane—the lavatory. Yelp, that's your domain too. Yours and literally every dude after he eats lunch. Yay!

Part 91 is supposed to be the pinnacle of flying. It almost always is. The clients are always the most particular and the most awful. To fly a nice family is considered the crème de la crème. Some single, thirsty-ass heauxes think flying with professional athlete teams is IT, but honestly, they usually get hit on the most by those dirty-ass coaches. We see you.

What we also see are the ball-less pilots that actually let a policy go down which states that they are not allowed to put any of the catering expenses on their cards. What a ridiculous premise for a business in the middle of a fucking pandemic. I mean, how awful do you have to be to people? That was a choice to put those kinds of ridiculous expenses on someone's PERSONAL CREDIT. Like, what the fuck? So many times companies like this then dispute charges. I once had an accountant who was doing work for Executive Jet Management at Berkshire Hathaway company actually REFUSE to pay almost $600 worth of expenses on a South Beach trip once. That was two days' work for me after taxes. Most of it was my food on the road. Some was catering expenses. This was the same year they claimed a $300 million profit for doing literally and absolutely nothing as said in a shareholders letter that quarter. This same company decided that they would limit flight crew meals for contractors to $65 a day. No matter if you are in New York City or Cleveland, let me tell you, that shit gets expensive. AGAIN asked to subsidize a wealthy clients desire to stay in South Beach a couple days. THIS IS ABSOLUTELY UNACCEPTABLE TO ASK FOR THE LOWEST PAID PERSON ON THE TEAM, WHO DOESN'T EVEN WORK FOR YOUR COMPANY FULL TIME TO PAY FOR YOUR CLIENTS FOOD, HOTEL, AND LITERALLY EVERYTHING THAT YOU REQUIRE OF THEM TO BE IN BUSINESS. WHERE DO YOU GET OFF?

CHAPTER 28

JOURNAL ENTRY #2

Presented raw and unedited for your amusement.

Sometime in 2021:

I had a memory the other day of actually wanting to become a Flight Attendant. It was never on commercial. Years ago, I looked into NetJets and sent them my naive resume. My blank ass, zero training, embarrassingly empty of aviation experience resume. I was so full of hope. I was way beyond full of hope. I was delusional and actually surprised when I didn't hear back from them.

I once had a boss say something to the effect of, everything you love in life has bullshit, it's just what kind of bullshit you can you tolerate.

That quote would haunt me for the rest of my career. Many times, after being berated, eating alone in my hotel room because I was too spent to entertain the pilots, I would wonder, *do I love this enough to tolerate its bullshit?*

I mean, I do have clients repeatedly request me. I'm routinely booked months in advance. Apparently, people enjoy my service and think I'm good at it.

I'm not sure we saw the same service because I feel like it could have been way better. I'm absolutely—no, excuse me—definitely certain in all aspects that it was my winning personality that got me through it. I think, in fact, that is most of life. If you can't get along with people, no one will want to work with you.

Sits here writing alone.

My service couldn't have been that bad. I mean, after flying this eagle-eyed billionaire for a mere three hours, I once got a job offer. After jokingly telling him they couldn't afford me. He told me to think about it and make him an offer.

I sat on it. Was this guy really serious? The next day, he rolled onto the jet asking where the offer was. I told him I was still marinating and wanted to see how their week played out.

When I finally emailed his company, I asked for $225,000. Which honestly seems absurd, and maybe was a little absurd, but I also had to end every single other contract I was working on, which after half a decade in aviation making contacts, I wasn't eager to do. The number had to reflect what I was giving up. I hit send on the email and held my breath thinking I was absolutely insane.

They emailed me back the next day with a $171K offer to work two weeks on, two weeks off. It was a good offer as far as money goes. It was an okay offer as far as the business model went. Also, it was exactly 25 percent below my asking price. That's part of the reason I didn't take it.

The other reason was, it was a known fact that you were probably gonna have the owner get a lil' handsy with you. That's not a direct quote, but its close enough to what the pilot carefully explained to me. Honestly, part of me feels like getting groped would have at least set up my bank account a tad. I mean, I don't want to and it makes me sick to my stomach. But… savings?

However, here I sit, savings account dwindling during a worldwide pandemic after my clients left me out in the cold. New York State government taking care of my pretty little hors d'oeuvres serving ass wondering, maybe I should have just let this powerful man feel me up just for a bit of financial security. Am I dumb? Maybe. Am I a borderline Narcoleptic Nancy, though? Also, yes.

Ultimately, it was the having to get up at 2 a.m. on Sundays for me.

Yikes. My body just dry-heaved at the mere thought of it. My adrenals themselves turned the offer down.

Also, though, they were paying well. They weren't paying *that* well for a billion-dollar company. You would expect them to want to be generous and set the tone for others. That is not in fact reality. Reality is greedy.

Greed everywhere, all the time, all at once.

Entitlement, all day every day. On yachts and planes, with cuisine and drinks. Who cares about that, though? That's just my ketchup-covered hands chiming in. The real gross-ass greed comes from how little they pay the people that make them so Goddamned rich in the first place.

Even Bill fucking Gates is selling a book for you to buy. Don't worry, it's only $35. THIRTY-FIVE DOLLARS? And he's worth how much again? A hundred trillion Bitcoin?

Geezus, why are you *selling* anything at this point? It's insatiable, pathological greed. How much money is enough, Billy? Is "enough" even attainable?

Heaping onto this steaming pile of greed is the fact that pilots would never dream of giving away their unpaid labor, but Flight Attendants are expected to. Everyone knows a pilot and a Flight Attendant in this type of situation.

In almost every other career, no one gives their time away. Yet, in the aviation world, it is routine that they will usually only pay you the day that you fly. Even though it routinely takes at least one additional day to plan and source what you need for their trip. If you land before midnight, they usually will not pay for the next day, even if you left the airport after midnight. Sometimes, you'll get a generous account that will pay you a day rate for the next day if you land after midnight. Which is not really that generous and only fair as there is a significant chance you wouldn't have been able to fly that next day anyway. It would have been very dicey to book that day to fly another unrelated trip knowing you could or would get in that late. If you couldn't be sure, you would have to cancel or not book that next day at all, just in case.

I know you want to talk daily rates you thirsty babes. I know it. Well listen, it can be good money. It can be *great* money, with certain accounts. It goes a lot farther when you're making a livable wage, though.

My most recent example of this would be an account who booked with me and canceled several times during the pandemic. If a trip cancels the day before, most companies will not pay you unless they cancel after 5 p.m. Then you will get paid a day rate (I heard that some companies will only pay half a day).

I had another company whittle several trips down to a three-day trip, then down to a single one-day trip. I had to swallow my pride and embarrassingly explain to the pilot who was booking me that unfortunately, as we're still mid-pandemic, it kicks me off of unemployment for the week, but it's not enough to make up the difference. Essentially, I would be unable to make rent, so I established a two-day minimum. His boomer response was, thanks for letting me know. He quite literally never reached out to me again, even though the clients requested me and the other pilots loved working with me.

I was fucking stunned. I mean, I'm coordinating catering the day before the trip for both the outbound and the inbound flights. Plus, like it's a pandemic, throw a sister a bone?!?! No? Turns out, hell no. I later looked at the trip sheet and to my absolute horror and disbelief saw that the plane was meant to land at 11:49 p.m. the night of the eighteen hour, day-long trip.

I shit you not.

So basically, what that meant for me is that I would have been on the plane until 1 a.m. and that extra time working, I would not be paid for. I would be donating that to the literal billionaire of a client. In addition to the eighteen hour work day, the entire day prior, I would have spent arranging catering and shopping for their specialty groceries and snacks. Absolutely pro-bono. Oh, and did I mention they were vegan?

I'm no mathematician, but let me lay this out for you. Basically, I would have to work T H R E E United States of America days in order to get paid for O N E day? My body literally ran cold as I wrote this sentence. The disrespect is truly hitting me. They must keep all that audacity in that wallet that's superglued shut.

I'm holding your hand when I say this, darling. There is no trickle down effect. That is a scam. The wealthy are usually stingy as fuck and they say, "That's how we stay this way." But like, it's so gross when it's at the expense of others being paid fairly.

And please, don't go all shoot the messenger on me. And don't misunderstand me. I'm not mad at people with money. I'm not even mad at anyone gaming the system. I'm mad at wealthy people gaming poor people. It's morally bankrupt, irrefutably ego centric, and wholly unnecessary.

How do you ask someone deemed an essential worker to run around the day before a trip, arranging catering during a pandemic no less, and then not pay her for it? What the actual Scrooge? Btw, if you didn't know this little tidbit, I am deadass serious. If you are a contract Flight Attendant, companies do not pay you for your days of labor before the trip starts. It is O U T R A G E O U S at best and a disgusting, filthy, patriarchal abomination because if more Flight Attendants were men, IT WOULDN'T BE HAPPENING AT ALL.

YES I AM YELLING.

I am mad as hell. This is so insane when I hear myself explaining it. These are the wealthiest people in the world and they are making middle class women work for free. FREE. Unpaid for a day's work. Insane.

Please do not get me wrong, the day pay is good. But for living in major cities in the United States, it's not amazing. And if you're among some of the wealthiest people on the planet and you're reading this, you should pay your motherfucking people, not see what you can get for free out of them.

SHAMEFUL.

The end.

CHAPTER 29

DRESS CODE

I can't actually believe I am contemplating if my work uniform—that I so painstakingly put together through trial-and-error washing in hotel bathroom sinks—is sexy enough.

What is "enough" anyway? I mean, my tits bust out of almost every shirt I own, so much so that an ex asked me why I always wore my tits out. Ever since then, I locked those bad boys away. That's abuse for ya. And now, here I am actually contemplating If I need to show them more. Like, what about if I comprised and just showed my collar bone? And what about my ass? There's zero hiding her. Shouldn't that be enough for a tip??? I mean, I bend over at least fifty times a flight, SURELY that would be enough for someone to throw me a hundo or two without me having to show a little more cleavage.

The nuances of this job are exhausting, let alone doing the actual work. Too sexy? Not sexy enough? Hoops too big? No hoops? Am I being *too* nice? Is there such a thing? Am I annoying the passengers? His wife looks annoyed. OMG I *AM* too sexy. There goes my tip. Wait, maybe he'll request me more when she's not flying? Unlikely. Maybe for a boys trip? Definitely.

Okay, so do I button all the way up? Or show a little clavicle and hope for a big fat tip like the one I'll inevitably give him in his pants when he sees this one inch square of skin I'm unveiling for this morning's flight of dudes. Should I wear THE skirt? You know the skirt. As ladies, we all have THAT skirt. The one that we bought because we feel HELLA CONFIDENT, HELLA sexy, and just overall like you could kick some righteous ass. That do-not-come-for-me-unless-I-send-for-you kind of attitude.

My particular skirt is a Spanx closet staple. It's a bomb-ass pencil skirt that hugs me in all the right places. It keeps flight bloat at bay with it's inherently Spanx "you will have a seamless flat tummy or I will squeeze you to death" mantra.

Okay, but like, now this is REALLY sexy. Pilates has been *working*, but this may be a whole new level at work.

Sexy has always come easily. It's almost the backdrop to my life, really. I always had to edit the sexy back. Really, I'm just being me and *you* are interpreting or finding it sexy. Either way, I've had to manage it like the star quality that it is. I learned to wield its power carefully and deliberately as to not scare off other women, wives, and potential beauty clients when I did skin care. I have to ward off unsavory pilot advances, client's wives insecurities, and now to procure tips? You'd think the prettier the girl, the easier her life is. Not the case. So many times someone will withhold from someone they deem to have more than them (looks, money, power) in an attempt to recalibrate the perceived power structure. Here I am this morning, attempting to hack the algorithm.

It's black. It's always black. All black everything because who knows what's going to land on me in flight. Any good New Yorker knows when in doubt black it out. All black everythang will get you in everywhere, everytime. So black it is. Always the same, really. Makes it easy and thoughtless. There are so many other moving parts that thinking about my outfit is literally the last thing on my mind. I cannot believe I uttered those words. Oh, how my life has changed. Turns out when your job is to serve others, you can lose yourself if you're not careful.

Slipping on my trusty Theory tux blazer over my peplum top and Spanx skirt, I can't stop thinking about what that pilot said about dressing sexier for tips. Damnit. My ass still juts out into the abyss like it's trying to sink the Titanic. Hazards of having T and A, a.k.a. that coveted hourglass coke bottle body, over-exaggerated by Barbie herself, has its pluses and minuses. Plus: I feel hot AF. Minus: I look hot AF—like maybe tooooo hot—for work. Plus, I am one confident bish in this ensemble. Minus, I am meant to please and serve and fade into the background. Plus: this hides any flight bloat. Minus: it's literally begging for someone to spank that Spanx ass. At this point, I haven't had a date in like a thousand consecutive days and would welcome a client to so much as heavily breathe on my arm, let alone slap my phat-ass. But obviously if he did, he better fucking tip that ass. Thank you.

Narrator: Her phat-ass would not be slapped that day, or any day on a jet.

Fuck what that pilot said, I'm thinking. I dress professionally and according to the day, schedule, weather, and work load. Period. *I do not dress for money*...as I put my clothes on...*to go to a job*...*that's going to pay me*.

Okay, fine. I do get dressed for money, but not like that. Maybe I should. Maybe that's the fucking problem. *OMG, get out of your head*, I think as I put black pants on and slip my black Rothy's on. All black everything, remember? Some girls wear white shirts and to that I say, better you than me, sister. I think it's important to know our strengths and me wearing white is not one of them.

Ugggghhhhh, fuck what that pilot said about dressing sexier for tips. I roll my eyes and button my black shirt to the top like a glossy, red-lipped IT nerd. So much for the tit tip.

CHAPTER 30

DATE RAPE

He was cute. He looked like one of my least favorite ex boyfriends which made me lurch a little at the thought. But, he was still cute. And you could tell he worked out. None of these things were particularly special to him. At the time, I flew a lot of professional athletes around, so good-looking rich guys were aplenty.

Unfortunately for them, I had a very hard and fast no dating clients policy. Which I am proud to say I stuck to 100 percent throughout all the years I flew. Do not get me wrong, there were men I absolutely fantasized about later, back in my hotel room. Curled toes and all. But, I never acted on it. Ever.

I lucked out though because this guy wasn't a client. He was a passenger, maybe twice, yes, but he was not a client of my boss's. Score. He sent his clients to my boss's clients, so this guy was completely on the table.

Looking back, there were a hundred red flags. I don't think he's a particularly bad guy. Let me preface this story by saying that. I do think he is the epitome of the patriarchal system wrapped up in one white boy. Retired athlete turned something in business for other athletes. Boring, but boy was he rich. He'd started a something or another and was currently making loads of money.

He'd struck up the conversation first, of course, because I am a delight and he could sense that from the beginning. He lingered behind as the rest of his party was deplaning so he could ask for my number in case they needed anything while on the ground. Wink wink. I told him my boss has it and he smiled and confessed it was for him.

Red flag. But, dammit, he's cute.

I oblige and he texts me as he's standing in front of me. Because that's what guys do these days, so even if you wanted to give them the wrong number, you can't.

His text popped up in front of him on my phone. Delighted, he tipped me and walked away.

Gimme that money, honey.

Not sure it was worth giving out my number, but he was very charming.

Red flag?

I clear up the plane and am kind of giddy actually. He's not flying back with us, so I likely won't see him again until he asks me out. Unless he flakes, in which case, I will see him the next time he flies with us. My stomach tightens. I hope he asks me out before that.

He texts me over the next week and I fortunately had time to meet up with him. He was a fabulous date. Funny, charming, complimentary, engaging. All the things. We even had a few friends in common. It truly was a fantastic date. Thinking back on it, I'm so disappointed in his behavior after that because I think we could have made a really good match. Alas, that was not to be our path.

When he did call, I wasn't surprised. I just had a feeling he would. I was surprised I actually had the time while I was in town between trips.

As the car he sent dropped me off in front of the hotel, I look down at my shoes thinking I wish I had worn a fuck-me heel.

Turns out it didn't matter because the date turned out to be a pretty fun and fantastic one, in spite of my lame shoe choice.

I did notice that he was drinking a lot. It's not abnormal, but the rate of the cocktails was noticeable to say the least. But weirdly, he seemed not to be getting drunk at all. I thought he was an absolute finance animal and had a high tolerance for skinny margaritas. Looking back, I think that man was doing blow in the bathroom like every other finance guy I know.

When he invited me back to his hotel to see the "best view of Manhattan," I laughed in his face, calling it "the best trick in Manhattan." Trying to persuade me to go by joking, it wasn't that at all. I did try to get out of it several times, even ribbing him about what a basic bitch move it was. He was insisting. He wasn't pulling me along or anything, but he wasn't accepting my many no thank you's either.

He knew I didn't have to fly the next day and was officially off, so there was no reason not to. Unless I didn't like him. Well-played, sir, well-played. I fell right into that and like a predicable pick-me, walked back to his apartment.

He made me a delicious 1942 poured over a large rock and started making out with me in his kitchen. Again.

We'd already made out at the downstairs bar in the hotel we'd had dinner in. They had this little photo booth and we had a hot make out sesh where he'd discovered I wasn't wearing any panties. I'm not a big ole minidress, pantiless whore, so hold your judgement, dear reader. My dress would not allow for such a garment to remain invisible. Fashion rule number one is and always will be NO PANTY LINES. The end. No arguing. Unless you're pregnant, then all bets are off baby girl, you do you.

A delighted grin formed on his face as he ran his grippy hands up and down my thighs and butt making sure there was nothing there. Then, in pure joy, he dipped me back and kissed me like the Goddess that I am.

It was pretty fucking hot. I mean, not that I'm reliving it as I'm writing this—I kind of want to keep that pretty little moment, all hot and sexy, untainted from his next moves. I find it hard to. But maybe one of you can use it for your own personal spank bank, and then sharing this story will bring me joy on several levels.

Still intrigued by the no panties life I'm living, he grabs me by the back of the head and passionately kisses me. It's super fucking hot. He's kissing my neck and puts his glass down as he whispers in my ear, "I'm not going to fuck you, I just want to taste you."

Excuse me? It was sploosh central. Yes, bitch get on your knees, is what I wanted to scream.

But before I could say a word, he had hiked up my dress and his face was drip central. I mean, this is not what I had wanted and this is why I didn't want to come back here. But, oh my God, it was good.

I was conflicted.

Condickted.

Ugggghhhhhh. Fuck, I should have just trusted my instincts.

So I grabbed the back of his head, okay mayyyybe I grinded slightly into his face before I pulled his lips off mine and asked for the much promised apartment tour.

But, wouldn't *you*??? I mean, it *was* hot. It was like way, way, *way* too early for that for me right now, but get it when you can, sometimes, ya know?

As I pulled away from him, and wriggled my dress down, he started showing me the art around his apartment. Unsurprisingly, we ended up in his bedroom. The whole room was full of floor-to-ceiling windows. The city lights of New York City sparkling and twinkling with the hustle of the city flying by. It was gorgeous, but I didn't walk in. He immediately told me to come in and not be afraid.

I laughed. Mostly because, as women, it's a nonthreatening way for us to react when we're uneasy or afraid.

He comes near me to guide me to the glass corner of the bedroom. It's a beautiful view he's saying, but I'm not really listening because this is where it always happens.

It. You ladies know what I'm talking about.

The Misunderstanding.

You know the one, where he wants to have sex, but you don't, so he tries anyway. It always is made to feel like some big Misunderstanding. But, it's not. We know it's not. That's why we always hate ourselves when it's over.

So there I am, trying to avoid the big Misunderstanding by suggesting we go up to see the views on the roof, like he'd wanted to.

Like he promised, remember?

He gently grabs my hand and turns me into him. He's actually so cute, I think. He's harmless. Right? He kisses me, passionately, hands all over me. Right.

Now he's kissing me somewhat aggressively, hands a little more handsy. I giggle because it's hot, but also because I'm a little uneasy.

All of a sudden, he tosses me to the bed and dives on top of me. It's still hot, but I'm way, way, *waaaay* uncomfortable, and as we're making out, I'm trying to let it cool off a little bit. You know, like using less tongue and pulling away for air, pushing his heaving chest away, trying to wiggle out from underneath his crushing pelvis. I'm giving all the signs of stop without making him feel insecure.

Insecure and embarrassed men can be dangerous men.

Even though he is pushing it too far. It's just an intense make-out session, so there's no need to all out reject him, I think.

Before I can even think of something gentle to say, he pops up off of me. I immediately attempt to get up. I'm pulling my dress down, but I'm kind of pinned on the bed with his legs. He's wrestling with his pants or something, but it's dark and he's backlit, so I can't see a thing.

Maybe his belt buckle was just pinching him, I reason. As this thought passes through my mind, he flops back down on top of me and rams his dick inside my dress, slides it all the way up my inner thigh, and up inside ME.

No consent.

No condom.

Straight beluga whale.

As I was already trying to get up, we had some momentum that helped me shove him out and off of me. As I scrambled with the awkwardness of it and stammered through the "I'm not ready yet." Um, um, um and he went through whatever the fuck he was saying. I don't even remember because I think I just heard like ringing in my ears. I feel like he stammered a small apology, like oh, oh, oh my bad. Like he didn't just jam his unrequested, unconsented dick inside someone. This same person, who in fact made a joke about you just trying to get her back to your apartment to score.

I vaguely remember him hustling me into the elevator after gifting me a tin with a joint wrapped in keef. Definitely wasn't worth getting raped for.

And it *was* rape, for the men out there who aren't clear. Just because a girl is into you, just because you're having a yummy or aggressive make-out session doesn't mean she wants to fuck you. Just because you're "seeing signs" doesn't mean she wants you to take the initiative.

It doesn't come off strong.

It doesn't come off sexy.

It's desperate.

If she wants it, she will tell you.

Let her take the lead. Especially the first time.

Why did I trust him?

Why didn't I just go home?

CHAPTER 31

THE SHRIMP LADY

My heartfelt rage was born out of absolute exasperation, frustration, some anger, but ultimately, despair of a predominantly patriarchal, always elitist system. Everyone has always said "Oh, work for the wealthy, the money will trickle down, you know." Classic Reaganomics bullshit.

For almost a year, this family had been trying to replace their very pregnant (and very much on maternity leave) Flight Attendant with yours truly. It was around Christmas when the owner himself approached me, and I gave him my salary request. I was excited to be finally having the conversation.

This next part I did not anticipate. He had already been briefed on my salary expectations. I knew that going into the chat. This is what made it all the more shocking.

"Your number is pretty high," he said, chuckling softly.

"Well, you get what you pay for," I shot back.

"Okay. But it's your decision to be single and live in Manhattan. I mean, what's stopping you from moving to New Jersey? There are cheaper places by the airport. Have you considered that?"

Have I considered leaving my life in the city to live in the middle of goddamn nowhere so he could save a few dollars?

"If you can't afford to pay me the salary I asked for," I said politely, "maybe *you* could move to New Jersey instead."

He chuckled again. Then agreed to my number.

In fact, he didn't. The salary he calculated included a yearly staff bonus that wasn't guaranteed, some per diem, health insurance, and a number of other expenses. The final salary ultimately came out to half of the original agreement.

The decently paid job dropped into being horrifyingly underpaid. I would have made more bartending. And I never would have considered working for this level of annoying clientele. But I was naive. I was hoodwinked.

The man who hired me has a wife. That ancient beaver is a difficult client. In some ways, she's fine. I like that she will tell you exactly what she wants. When it comes to food, she's very specific.

I like it less that she's very hands on.

You *will* serve to her exact specifications, because if not, she's coming back into the galley to do it herself. You will be demoted to sous-chef. You will become her prep bitch. She might allow you to throw a shrimp or two on her plate, but she's absolutely rearranging them. It's a lot to deal with.

One of our more harrowing interactions played out like this:

Someone is stomping down the cabin corridor. *Oh my God, this bitch has really come back here again.*

I lean around the wall to see her gangly body attempting to walk back into the galley. After decades of eating like a newt, her walking is painfully labored and her legs frail. She is holding onto the seats, kind of lurching from one row to the next.

She knows I'm preparing lunch for her and her guests and she wants in. Sorry, wait, that's not accurate. She wants to come back and micromanage the living fuck out of me. She's not alone in the eating disorder category or the control tendencies. Most rich wives are like this. There must be a link between being super fucking skinny and absolutely drippingly loaded.

She wants in on the shrimp and sashimi action. She's going to tell me to put three pieces of sashimi on her plate. I will. She's then going to tell me to put one shrimp on. Actually, make it two, she'll say. She's splurging.

I see her out of the corner of my eye. As I greet her, she asks me to put a shrimp on her plate. She pauses, actually make it two. I laugh internally. I smile externally. This is in the height of those glorious pre-mask days, so she can see I am genuinely delighted by our interaction.

As I add the second shrimp alongside his homie and two pieces of beet red salmon that she also requested, I see her cramming a third into her mouth. It must be a special occasion. She hurries me along as I follow behind her. Once seated, she looks at the plate.

With the deadest dead pan that ever did dead pan she whines, "Ohh myyyyyyy Danielle, I couldn't possibly eat TWO WHOLE PIECES of sashimi. What are you *thinking*? Take one away immediately."

TAKE ONE AWAY. This is a common request of hers. The mere thought of the offending item even being C L O S E to the client is an imposition in the least and an absolute abomination at present. Geezus, I could not disdain working for this woman any more. Like, how about you just don't eat it, don't look at it, just ignore it? It's going in the garbage anyway. Like, can't it just sit there?! What is the harm???

I am seriously asking.

Honestly, every industry has clients that suck, but OH MY GOD this level of snobbery can be the fucking worst sometimes. I have many wealthy friends that are the epitome of kindness and realness and compassion and generosity and everything you would imagine a happy wealthy person to be. That's the oxymoron right there, though. Happy Wealthy people are few and far between. This industry collects the unhappy ones like you collect those dusty-ass Louis Vuitton carryall bags.

So obviously, I take the plate away as one of her guests sheepishly looks at me. So often these women perform in front of their guests. It's a dance of power. Often times, their guests don't even notice. It's actually more uncomfortable when they do. Then you see them for who they really are. They know that client is a piece of human garbage, but they are willing to put up with it for a ride on the jet, baby. Living the glam life with their friend. Their friend who's a raging cunt. And they know it.

It's wild that it never really bothers me in the moment. It's my duty to make my clients as comfortable as possible. Even the ones who only take comfort in torturing me. I genuinely enjoy helping people and take pride in it. Being a caretaker is built into the nature of being a great Flight Attendant.

In moments like this sashimi situation, I turn it up to eleven and snap off the dial. There's no way she'll see me sweat. And despite my chronic complaining after the fact, the goal is always to make clients—even someone like her—look good in front of their friends. It's a reflection on the people who hired me, and the ones who own the plane.

It's only after the fact when I'm retelling a story like this that I even realize what embarrassing behavior it is. If shame were still a thing, she *would* be embarrassed.

Truth be told, I'd like to tell her that adults have no business acting like this. She should be like Jack's giant bean stalk and grow up.

If you are one of these people that makes your server or Flight Attendant take something off of your plate that isn't an allergy, I say this with love: Fuck you twice.

Oh whoops, I mean fuck you thrice.

CHAPTER 32

FAST FOOD

It doesn't matter how much catering you order, the passengers will, beyond a shadow of a whiff of a doubt bring something with them that they want you to feed them, store for them, freeze for them, or put in the cooler for them.

Sometimes, you even get the privilege of picking it up for them in addition to the $4K of specialty catering you purchased for an intimate entourage of six. This small of a crew only included the essential staff. That would be the Lead themselves, of course, their massage therapist, manager, full-time assistant, photographer, and "friend" assistant. That's the unpaid sucker that follows the celeb around because of all the fun perks, but gets treated like staff, berated and/or hissed at on a daily basis just to maintain the power structure. This "friend" assistant is usually from the same hometown, but they don't have to be. They could be a newish friend from within their industry or a total weirdo stranger who is basically a super fan.

I digress.

The Lead inevitably always wants something else last minute. Usually these requests can be accommodated because Uber

Eats is the champion of picking food up that you don't have time for. They love a ridiculous last minute request, almost as much as they love treating you like you're a proxy to their assistant, but not as much as they love signing a napkin as your "tip." The mentality is, the trip is sponsored by the production company, so why should they come out of their own pockets at work? Ugh, I know so many of us have worked hospitality industry jobs and know that IRL it can be gross and disturbing, so I hope you're still wearing your seatbelt. It gets grosser.

LA celebs are the same coming through with that last minute In-N-Out request. Let me ask you LA babies about this. When was the last fucking time you went to In-N-Out burger near Van Nuys and got out of there in less than ninety minutes? The answer is "never" because it is such an insanely vapid time suck.

They have literally three assistants and a TEAM of people sending you on a worldwide tour, they could absolutely have asked one of them to pick up their greasy In-N-Out during rush hour in LA for the love of all that is holy? Have a driver do it. Pick a team member. The Flight Attendant is not that team member. By the time they placed that last minute request, I'd already ordered their deconstructed dino nuggies off their bitchy ass seventh-level-of-hell rider.

Just so everyone is clear, the Flight Attendant's job, first and foremost, is a safety position. Second to that, it is to make a flight comfortable. Not *enjoyable.* As much as I wish, I cannot be a boundless wellspring of joy (there's need a pill for that, darling). This means I prep a fifty-million-dollar jet with Frette bedding for a lucky seven and handle cunt-level catering for twenty. Catering that won't be eaten anyway. It's one of the worst parts of the job. Like ma'am, I am qualified to drag your plastic face out of a burning plane and am attempting to ready a jet cabin for an eleven-hour camping trip in the air to fucking Japan. Now, you're sending my sweet tits out for fucking burgers during LA rush hour? Like, *yeah* I want a burger, but now is *not* the time. Get a clue.

This Lead did not, in fact, get a clue. Consequently, this teensy In-N-Out quick burger run request took me two of the three hours I had to ready the plane. The client didn't make the request until I had been on the plane for a half hour already, so I literally showed up minutes before the international celebrity on a plane I had only spent thirty sweaty minutes on. Every corporate Flight Attendant reading this is cringing because this is an absolute nightmare scenario.

I am not saying that we should not be doing the food. Let me be clear when I state that it is absolutely, exactly our job. If you don't do food, you don't do Private Jets, honey. Get off the plane. In fact, you never even made it onto the plane if you were one of my girls. No chance.

So, In-N-Out is a VERY popular request. Happy to pick it up for you and grab the crew a few burgers too. We can handle anything, but a little prep goes a LONG way. Please remember that when you're dealing with your Flight Attendants. Or just use Uber Eats, Caviar, I dunno, but don't last minute request something at dinner time from the most popular joint in town from the Flight Attendant that's already at the plane. Like, think of someone other than yourself.

Just kidding. That's *not* a celebrity's job.

They are the talent. No one else matters. That's how they got to the top, baby!

The second most popular onboard request is Popeyes Chicken. That spicy chicken sandwich? Perfection. Love it.

Happy to scarf one down myself. All I can say, though, is DO NOT eat Popeyes and fly. It has never in the history of Popeyes or aviation been an enjoyable combo. This is the helium balloon of snacks at forty thousand feet. This will always end up in what is unaffectionately called bubble guts.

This entourage of entertainment guys are overnighting (surprise surprise) to some bumfuck snooze-ville middle of nowhere location for a show. That's showbiz for you. They haven't sent catering, but they order the same thing every flight, so I have some options for them. Then, as I'm feverishly checking my email for any last minute fires to put out, the fated email comes through.

Plot twist: They want Popeyes.

I'm not entirely sure how these guys eat at home, but their rider shows a bunch of healthy-ish options. I feel like Popeyes is kind of a treat for them. So I'm pumped to indulge them. I get nothing for myself, even though that spicy chicken sandwich is making me drool at the thought. I'm super particular about what I eat before I fly. Being bloated in the air sucks. Having gas in the air sucks. Farting in the air is SUCH a relief. But having the BGs is awful. It feels like a fat bloated snake thrashing around inside your belly.

This group? Scarfs it down.

I'm making second plates, they're licking their fingers, they're talking shit to each other, maybe even me too a little bit and everyone is laughing and having a good time. I know they're going to pass the fuck out any minute so I'm getting blankets ready, refilling drinks, and putting pillows at their seats.

As I'm dimming the lights and cleaning up the cabin for them to rest, it starts.

Pppppppffffffffffffffffffpppp.

The whole cabin erupts in equal amounts laughter and grumbling. Everyone starts throwing shade at whoever that little rip came from.

Pppppppffffffffggggggggggggggfgfffpfppppppfpfpfpfpf.

Um, whoa. That one's gonna be ripe for sure. The worst thing about the stanky ones are that the air blows out directly into the pilot's face on this aircraft. They are swallowing a whole face full of Popeyes ass right now.

NOT SO FUN FACT

The entire jet knows when you're blowing up the bathroom. Bonus, if you're in a Gulfstream, the lavatory air blows directly into the pilots' faces.

Soon the cabin is filled with rancid booty and grown men yelling at each other, blaming the battery acid inside them. It quickly becomes a free-for-all of roast-level insults being thrown back and forth. The smell is so putrid that these guys are getting furious with each other. Worse still, is even after everyone falls asleep, the undie thunder keeps coming.

Some are so bad that they are waking each other up. Either by the sound or the sheer repulsive stench. It is absolute stank chaos in the dark. Halfway through the night, there is a particularly juicy and stanky rip that I'm pretty sure blows right through this guy's pants. It wakes one of the dudes up and he is so fucking pissed about it he got up and starts pillow fighting his passed-out friend, calling him every name under the sun—everything but a child of God. I mean, the man couldn't help it, he was sleeping, but oh my God the smell almost suffocates us all.

All I can think about is if we had it this bad in the back, the poor, poor pilots must be in their oxygen masks up front.

CHAPTER 33

STOCKHOLM SYNDROME

Apparently, when we were children, I used to speak for James. According to our mother, I somehow knew what he was saying. Fast forward to adulthood and it's funny how life works out.

After becoming increasingly numb to making the most mundane of requests perpetually wrong and being constantly scolded for them, we realized I had Stockholm Syndrome. I could no longer distinguish the insane requests from the commonplace. They had all merged into one amalgamous blob of entitlement.

I, along with every other corporate flight attendant, have become blind to the insanity of our work.

Twenty-seven glass bottles of juice for one person on a forty-two-minute flight?

My question would be, why would I have anything *less* on board?

My brother would say, "That is four hundred and thirty-two ounces of liquid, darling. No one could consume that on an eleven-hour flight to Japan, let alone a forty-two-minute hop from LA to Vegas."

And he was right.

Truly, I thank every god on planet Earth for him. He is the yin to my yang, the Salt to my Peppa.

I never would have survived without him.

I was retelling what I was convinced was a hilarious anecdote about the seven surprise Starbucks Frappuccinos made on board. Yet, as I waited for the assumed incoming laugh at the end of my tale, it...wasn't there?

James was absolutely appalled. He pointed out the weirdly obvious, almost sexual power trip of the old fossil. The man springs a midair, bespoke and trademarked specialty drink that had never been mentioned or found on his rider for the entirety of our time together.

"Seven times? That's fucking diabolical," he said.

And there James was, right again.

I thought about it. Not only had he never made this request before, his wife wasn't on board for his little power trip. His male assistants, however, were all watching me flounder and beg for the approval of their decrepit skeleton of a hedge fund boss. All while the bald badger was smiling and relishing in every second of it.

I'd thought the worst part was that he only had a sip. All that Frappuccino foreplay for nothing. The real nightmare was that I had become accustomed to this kind of treatment.

And that's the day James became my translator.

GET OFF THE PLANE

As Flight Crew, the second the jet stops moving, we are saying a prayer for you to get the fuck off the jet.

It sounds so dumb, like what's another hour or so of getting everyone off the jet and into cars. But, for the love of Baby Christo, we've been focusing on your trip for, at minimum, twenty-four to forty-eight hours and we are ready for it to be over. Plus, I bet you're not going to tip, either? Big sigh. Surprise surprise. Get off even faster. And I hope you forget those cute sunglasses.

But there's always that client that fancies themselves a professional poker player and wants to play just one more annoying game of poker. The funny part is, they are usually paying for everyone's salary and then playing for that money BACK.

The way these guys would play poker against their employer with their own salary is hilarious. Sometimes they would play for another hour or so on the jet, just for their boss to take money back from his own entourage. Laughable. Sometimes he would want to play for such large sums of cash that he would have to front the cash for everyone to play. Only to take most of it away from them. Insane. Certifiably egomaniacal.

At times, members of the entourage would be losing so badly that they would throw the table, cards going everywhere, laughter ensuing from everyone else, while the loser demands the bottle of Crown Apple and throws his thousands on the ground in a big boy tantrum. As hilarious as it was, I still wanted them to get off the fucking jet. It sucked seeing cash fly everywhere while none of it landed on me. Watching them scramble to grab hundreds, though, was pretty satisfying in a fuck-the-rich kind of way. They had no idea how crappy their behavior was, just like everyone else in these stories.

I hope these true trauma dumpy tales were as appalling for you to read as they have been for me to live and for James to experience in real time.

Maybe I sound like an asshole for sharing all these, and maybe I am. After all, we all have a shadow self that none of us can escape from. Names have been redacted not just to protect us from the malevolent, but to remind us all that sometimes being an asshole is a universal experience. And that if you don't see the asshole, sometimes the asshole is you.

ABOUT THE AUTHORS

Danielle Styron is an American-British Glamazon who grew up a nomad, complete with international schools and Middle Eastern Royalty. After graduating from James Madison University, she dabbled as a graphic designer and model before obtaining an Aesthetics license.

Upon arriving in Manhattan, Danielle's genuine Pollyanna spirit and million-watt smile earned her a coveted spot as a private flight attendant. She quickly became a highly requested and beloved in-flight Diet Coke confidant, burying secrets and putting out fires for some of the world's most recognizable names in entertainment and business.

Today, Danielle can be found nestled in her sanctuary in New York City. Or Westport, maybe. Or try the Four Seasons in Anguilla; she likes it there.

James Styron graduated from James Madison University where he went on to live a hundred lives as a wine broker, a bartender, an acro-aerialist, a medical biller, a textile salesman, a project manager, and a visual coordinator in the NYC fashion industry. He returned to his true passion—writing—at the behest of his sister, turning her trauma journals into *The Mile High Club*.